Christian Hymns Observed

When in Our Music God is Glorified

Erik Routley

Prestige Publications, Inc.
Princeton, New Jersey 08540

© 1982 Prestige Publications, Inc.
International Copyright Secured. All Rights Reserved.
Printed in the United States of America.
Library of Congress Catalog Card Number: 82-061841
ISBN Number: 0-911009-00-0

FOREWORD

The sudden and untimely death of Erik Routley on October 8, 1982, just as this volume was about to go to press, ended the brilliant and prolific career of one of the leading authorities on the music of the church. His writings on Christian hymnody, covering some ten books and numerous articles, are recognized as among the most important contributions to the literature. His first published work on this topic was penned during his student days at Oxford and appeared in 1950 under the title *The Church and Music* (Duckworth, 1950, revised 1967). *Christian Hymns Observed,* completed by the author in December 1980, brought to a close a writing career that produced a total of forty published works, including the hymnals which he edited and to which he contributed. Because many of Dr. Routley's achievements as a writer are largely unknown to the general reader, it is the purpose of this foreword to shed light on some of these accomplishments.

Erik Routley was born in Brighton, England, on October 31, 1917, the only child of John and Eleanor Routley. He was nurtured in the south of England by a family in which religion and culture were considered important. Following private elementary education in his home town, he was sent to Lancing College, a preparatory school in Sussex, for his preparatory schooling. In 1936, at the age of nineteen, he went to Oxford to study classics at Magdalen College, earning the Bachelor of Arts degree in 1940 and the Master of Arts degree in 1943. He remained at Oxford for this theological studies which were completed in 1946 at Mansfield College. The Doctor of Philosophy degree (D.Phil.), earned in 1952, completed his formal education. His doctoral thesis was subsequently published as *The Music of Christian Hymnody* (Independent Press, 1957).

For a period of thirty-one years (1943-1974), Erik Routley served as a minister in the Congregational Church (then known as the Congregational Union of England and Wales). His pastorates included Wednesbury (1943-45), Dartford (1945-48), Edinburgh (1959-67) and Newcastle upon Tyne (1967-74). In the eleven year period between Dartford and Edinburgh, he returned to Oxford to fill an academic appointment at Mansfield College as lecturer in church history, chaplain, director of music and librarian. After returning to England following a thirteen year pastorate at the Augustine-Bristo Church in Edinburgh, Scotland, he was elected President of the Congregational Church in England and Wales (1970-71). When the Congregational Church became a part of the United Reformed Church in 1972, he was appointed chairman of the Doctrine and Worship Committee of this new denomination.

While his first professional appointment in music did not occur until 1975, when he emigrated to the United States, Dr. Routley's keen interest in the music of the church was evident even during the early years of his parish ministry. In 1944, while still in Wednesbury, he was named general secretary and a member of the editorial board for the hymnal *Congregational Praise* (1953). His first hymn tunes appeared in this publication. He was appointed editor of the *Bulletin* of The Hymn Society in 1948 and continued in this capacity until he moved to America.

The Oxford years (1948-59) were happy and productive for Erik Routley as he saw his first eleven books published, including the two theses mentioned above, the completion of *Congregational Praise* and the *University Carol Book* (1961), and experienced the intellectual stimulation of working in the highly-charged academic environment of Oxford University. The Edinburgh period, which followed, proved to be equally prolific as thirteen additional books were published between 1959 and 1967, including the influential *Twentieth Century Church Music* (Jenkins, 1964), a volume which eventually became his most popular book on both sides of the Atlantic. In 1965, he was made a Fellow of the Royal School of Church Music (FRSCM); the first non-Anglican to be so honored.

The year 1967 brought a call from St. James Church in Newcastle upon Tyne, and he returned to England for what was to be his final pastorate. It was during the seven year Newcastle period that six of his books were written, including *The Musical Wesleys* (Jenkins, 1969), *Saul Among the Prophets* (Epworth, 1971; published in America by The Upper Room, 1972), *The Puritan Pleasures of the Detective Story* (Gollancz, 1972), and *Exploring the Psalms* (Westminster 1975). The delightful volume on the detective story prompted the English Crime Writers' Circle to invite him to address them at one of their regular meetings. These years also saw his involvement with two other hymnals, *Hymns for Celebration* (RSCM, 1974) and *Cantate Domino* (World Council of Churches, 1974). One other kind of musical recognition came to Dr. Routley during his last year at Newcastle upon Tyne; he was elected President of the Incorporated Association of Organists of Great Britain, but did not take office because of his move to America.

Prior to coming to the United States on a permanent basis, he had visited America ten times, including lecture tours in 1962, 1966, 1969, 1971 and 1973. The 1966 visit was especially significant in that two of his books on church music grew out of lectureships at American seminaries: the Stone Lectures at Princeton Theological Seminary produced *Words, Music and the Church* (Abingdon, 1968) while the Gheens Lectures at the Louisville Baptist Seminary resulted in *Music Leader-*

ship in the Church (Abingdon, 1967). During the 1971 tour he was made a Fellow of Westminster Choir College (FWCC).

The eight years in the United States proved to be a time of both influence and productivity. As professor of church music and director of the chapel at Westminster Choir College Erik Routley was immediately recognized as a national figure in church music. Hardly a week went by that he was not invited to preach, lecture, lead a hymn sing or participate in a church music workshop somewhere throughout the country. He had been in America only a few months when he was asked by the President of Westminster Choir College to compile a hymn supplement for the chapel. The result was *Westminster Praise* (Hinshaw, 1976). Soon he was also at work on three other hymnals: *Ecumenical Praise* (Agape, 1977), *Songs of Thanks and Praise* (Hinshaw, 1980) and *Rejoice in the Lord* (completed before his death and scheduled for release in 1984 by the Reformed Church in America).

This Princeton period also resulted in a number of books, including *A Short History of English Church Music* (Mowbray, 1977), *Church Music and the Christian Faith* (Agape, 1978), and the two volume *Panorama of Christian Hymnody* (Liturgical Press, 1979). One of his more unusual works was released in 1980, a "talking" book of six hours length on cassette entitled *Christian Hymns: An Introduction to their Story* (Prestige, 1980).

While there have been a number of books concerned with the hymns of the Christian church, there are not many that combine real originality with intellectual integrity. Yet it is exactly this combination that makes *Christian Hymns Observed,* Erik Routley's final statement on Christian hymnody, such a valuable addition to the literature. Simply because he studied the subject for fifty years, he could open the book with the statement "hymns are delightful and dangerous things," and then close it with these words: "But where a hymn in a service of worship beckons to the worshiper at his or her best and causes that worshiper to feel or say, 'That is what I wanted to say, but I am grateful to whoever put the words in my mouth,' then it has done its work." Erik Routley has indeed done his work. This short book will be cherished for years to come by those who want a fresh and yet comprehensive approach to the subject of Christian hymnody.

Ray Robinson
President
Westminster Choir College

PREFACE

I suspect that the suggestion that I should write a short book about hymns was made by my good friend Ray Robinson in pursuit of a bet with some third party: the odds against its being possible would have been handsome.

But here it is. Patient people who have waded through all the pages I have written on this subject, or have turned away in resignation from the intolerably expensive tomes that have formed a recent part of my garrulous output, will wonder what would be the purpose of offering this one, and whether there's anything new to say.

Well, a short book about hymns is obviously possible — others have done it very well — but I find it difficult to confine such a book to a mere recitation of the story because it would look rather like a telephone directory without the numbers — long lists of names with room for precious little else. I thought perhaps that didn't need doing again.

But there is just one point which I think worth making, and which I haven't seen made elsewhere, concerning the reasons why people have sung hymns in the different ages, which in a book that is little more than an extended essay I think can be made. So I am offering a little tract, as it were, with as few footnotes as possible, and as few numerical references as we can manage with, mentioning nothing like all the great hymns or great hymn writers, but, as I hope, giving the general shape of the story and hanging the facts on a theme which I want to develop.

I do this because I am increasingly conscious that what is needed for the improvement of hymnody just now is not exhaustive knowledge but an insight into what happens when people sing them. To compare notes with the people of past ages can be very useful: it helps to provide a foundation for some contemporary and critical comments I have to make near the end. The reader who wants more facts can find them in plenty of other books: the reader who wants a more complete detailed history can borrow a copy of my book, *A Panorama of Christian Hymnody,* or, if very affluent, even buy it. But I hope it isn't out of place to offer here a more informal book which is to some extent a personal testimony.

I have been studying this subject on and off for fifty years, and formally teaching it for five. Those unfortunate students who have passed into (and thankfully out of) my classes will all tell you that as a teacher I break every rule in the book: mainly because I haven't read the book. My principle, if that's not too strong a word, is that if a teacher is idiosyncratic, prejudiced, and (what's the word they love to use? —) 'opinionated', at least the victims have something to complain about and can readily identify it. This process usually gives pleasure. Well —

you, the reader, won't be left in any doubt about my opinions, and I can already see the reviewers sharpening their knives in preparation for the carve-up they will feel obliged to administer about those opinions. But I do claim that the point I chiefly want to make is an important one; I think the argument is valid; and I think it hasn't been made in just this way before.

I can't promise that this is my last book on hymns: how good it would be if it were! It's possible that what I learn from critics may cause me to write another that corrects this one. But if you want a quick helicopter ride around the buzzing metropolis that is hymnody, you may fasten your seat belt now.

E.R.
Princeton, NJ
December 1980

CONTENTS

I

The Nature of Hymnody

Hymns are delightful and dangerous things. They are regarded, in the late twentieth century, as inseparable from the worship of all but a very few Christian groups. They are as familiar an activity as reading a newspaper: in worship they are for many people the most intelligible and agreeable of all the activities they are invited to join in or to witness; they are the most easily memorized of all Christian statements, and one who has not been in a church for most of a lifetime, but who was brought up in church when young, remembers some hymns, though everything else may be forgotten.

Hymns are a kind of song: but they differ from a professional song, or an art-song, in being songs for unmusical people to sing together. They are a kind of poetry, but they are such poetry as unliterary people can utter together. The music carries the poetry into the mind and experience; and if the poetry is too weighty for the music to get it moving, it won't move; while if the music is so eloquent as to drown the sound of the words, the words, no matter what nonsense they may talk, will go clear past the critical faculty into the affections.

Hymns, being communal song, have a good deal in common with folk song. So let us for a moment consider folk song. Folk song is that kind of song which people sing without any concern with who its composer was, or of the age from which it came: that is, without critical concern and without the kind of appreciation a professional brings to the contemplation of music. True: many folk songs are recognized by cultivated musicians as being of great beauty —but whereas some kinds of music can speak only to those who are well trained in music's language, true folk song speaks to all.

Secular folk song goes with words concerned with the things that mean most to a community: basically these are love, work and death. Folk song universalizes these experiences; it objectifies them, and by so doing detaches the singer from the anxieties which all three inevitably carry; the music and the verse smooth the asperities of the basic experiences of life, make them friendly and tractable. A folk song can handle anything from high humor to high tragedy but when it does that, it makes life's incongruities and anomalies entertaining by transforming them into humor, and life's griefs less oppressive by allowing the singer to stand away from them and, obscurely no doubt but none the less assuredly, to feel that the burden is shared by humanity.

One form of folk song is the work song — the sea shanty, let us say: the song adapted to the rhythms of hauling up sails or turning a capstan. Such songs have now gone into history with the disappearance of sails and capstans: but the rhythm of the song, and the narrative of the crude verse, laced with bawdiness quite often, together with the burden, or chorus, in which everbody who had breath to spare could join, eased the rigor of the work and made its drudgery friendly: that is a parable of what all folk song ever did, whether or not it was associated with muscular and physical work.

When we speak of folk song now we still mean songs which have survived through many generations and whose origins are buried in mystery. But of course there are folk songs whose origins are perfectly discoverable and may be quite recent. As soon as a song becomes the property of people who are not musical, as soon as it can be sung, and is sung, by people who are not in any sense natural singers (still less professional ones) it is a folk song. It happens that our present age is so sated with so vast a deluge of public music that it is difficult for any song to rise to the top — the crowd jostles too much further down: people whistle a good deal less than they used to. But right up to the days of the First World War folk song flourished in this sense. It could be fashioned out of what began as 'serious' music, like 'Land of Hope and Glory'; it could emerge from goodness knew where, like 'Pack up your troubles': it could be composed by an identifiable composer like Stephen Foster. Indeed, there were, during the early age of new-style popular music, plenty of tunes of Noel Coward's that came close to achieving folk-song status — and of Cole Porter's. It is an accident — one hopes, a recoverable one, though nobody can be optimistic about that just now — that the music with which ordinary folk are bombarded in modern society is either so sophisticated and ingenious in its vulgarity, or associated, as are the ubiquitous commercials of the advertising media, with such dubious purposes, that ours happens to be an age in which it is necessary to explain the nature of folk song at all.

But there is no question that some hymns have achieved folk-song standing. 'Amazing Grace', for example: this is now a secular folk song, in as much as it is often sung in contexts in which the import of the phrase 'Amazing Grace' has no meaning and by people who have, and want to have, no conception of what they are singing about. The same could be said of 'Morning has broken', another casualty of the media-age, — though apart from the fact that it seems to be heard quite acceptably at any time of day or night, one has to admit that its text doesn't lose much if nobody attends to it. The association of 'Abide with me' and the Welsh tune 'Cwm Rhondda' with football matches (and they are now usually solos or choral numbers rather than joined in by all present on such occasions) has given them a folk-song standing.

It looks then from what we have just said as if we are going to argue that folk song is a poor relation of hymnody, or of poetry and music in general; we have said, and we shall indeed insist on saying, that the hymns we have mentioned have been debased, and in some cases fatally damaged, by becoming folk songs. But in fact we are going to say something quite different, and we must at once clear up what will otherwise be a confusion and a contradiction.

Hymns are the folk song of the Christian folk. But the Christian folk is a very odd creature indeed. Recall what we said a minute ago. Folk song celebrates what means most to the folk. That is true of hymns. So if you know what hymns a person loves most, or what hymns a congregation is most addicted to, you will be able to infer what, in Christianity, means most to that person or that church. And that inference won't be speculative: it will be perfectly sound.

You are entitled to say that when people sing hymns they don't pay much attention to the words they sing, and that their satisfaction is usually generated by the tune rather than the text. In as much as that is true, it is a degeneration (as we shall show) from an earlier state of things: but if we have to accept it, then we shall be obliged to judge the content of a person's or a group's faith by the music perhaps more than by the words they sing in their hymns. So be it; it makes life a little more difficult because the judgment we have just said is a valid one requires some musical expertness before it can be made. But the fact is that words still mean a good deal; or if they don't, once the music has carried them past the critical faculty into the affections, they do a certain amount of good or harm.

Notice at this point two odd things about this kind of folk song. In the first place, there are sensitive people who have declared their extreme dislike of hymns: the most eloquent and eminent of these is the late C.S. Lewis to whom we shall return later; but the whole Quaker tradition, which is a culture of responsible, orderly and sensitive minds, is against communal hymn singing in their central acts of worship. 'Hymn-singing' or 'psalm-singing', used as an adjective, was at one time a very commonly accepted epithet of abuse as applied to the pious. Associated with this is the other point: hymn-lovers and hymn-critics often speak of bad hymns as distinguished from good ones. Who ever spoke of a bad sea-shanty, or a bad medieval carol? (One species of folk-song, the nursery-rhyme, has evoked from enlightened educationists criticisms in this or that case of a rhyme, like 'Dong Dong Bell, Pussy's in the well', which they deem to be conducive to unacceptable moral standards in young children: but that is an unusual case and statements of it are usually loaded with a good deal of overkill: there are people who would say we shouldn't sing the Twenty-Third Psalm because it is insulting to call people sheep).

Something has come into sight which we must identify. There is some quality about *Christian* folk songs that makes them vulnerable to corruption in a sense in which secular folk-songs aren't.

Well: the fact (which few people have noticed, or anyhow commented on) is that Christianity is as fatally *imitable* as the music of Handel. Any musician knows how in the English eighteenth century music took on a fatal facility and garrulousness which it took a Vaughan Williams to identify, diagnose, and dissipate. That was, it is hardly unfair to say, because everybody thought they could write like Handel (or, on the continent, like the pupils of Bach). There was a new market for it, and the hacks were ready to meet the demand. In the same way there have always been imitations of Christianity (which had in common with the real thing only those aspects of the real thing which appeal to the unregenerate nature) that have never failed to win a measure of popular approval. I shall be obliged to refer later on to the evangelical tyranny of Count Nicolas von Zinzendorf, and I shall have to cause my readers and myself the embarrassment of referring to contemporary versions of that. There have been power-seeking imitations of Christianity, and moralistic imitations, and pseudo-mystical imitations, and pseudo-poetic imitations, and organization-minded imitations, and even ecumenical imitations — and they all have this in common with each other, that any attempt to criticize them is always made to reflect on the critic, and to justify the attribution to him of looseness of faith, hostility to the truth, and a general beastliness of nature. They also have this in common — that they have parted company with reason, and that they have renounced penitence: but it is never any use saying so. It is, one has to say, fatally easy to imitate or travesty Christianity.

Well, hymnody is the folk-song of *that* — of the Faith in all its austerity and grandeur here, and of the imitation in all its attractiveness there. We have to take it as we find it, and obviously in a short book it will be sensible to concentrate on what seems to reflect the authentic innocent beauty of the Christian faith and style. But we may as well know what we are in for.

Hymn singing is nowadays thought of as a communal or congregational activity, and we should be disposed to define a hymn as a strophic song on a Christian subject capable of being sung by a congregation

4

which was not in any sense made up of trained singers. But any definition in terms of that kind would be narrower than the original definition of a hymn, which is simply a song of praise. 'Hymn' is a Greek word, in use long before the Christian era. A hymn need not, on that primitive definition, be religious and it need not be communally sung: therefore obviously it need not be strophic. It is no more than a song of a serious kind making use of poetry and music in a way which tends to exalt the mind of the singer and listener towards lofty subjects — whatever subject may be recognized by that particular community as lofty. In Christian use, 'Hymn' has not necessarily meant a congregational song: indeed for three quarters of the time that Christianity has been in the world it meant, as we shall see in a moment, precisely not that. And even during the time when congregational singing was familiar in church (that is, after the Reformation) 'Hymn' can mean a choral piece performed to a listening congregation.

It is as well to remember that, even though the subject of this book is in fact congregational hymnody. For as long as hymnody is not the property of an uncritical congregation, it is subject only to the disciplines of music and poetry and, if it is Christian, Christian theology. As soon as it falls into the hands of people whose chief business is not thinking about poetry and music, it tends to require other forms of discipline, and from time to time the Church has applied it, with greater or less success.

But in more recent times — broadly speaking, during the century now nearing its end — the idea of 'a good hymn' and 'a bad hymn', the self-conscious criticism and investigation of hymns according to the disciplines of literature, music and theology, has become an accepted study, and that is known as hymnology. There has always been criticism of the use of music in church, and authorities from time to time have warned the church against its incongruous, unseasonable or extravagant use: that is not hymnology because what is said in such warnings can just as well be said about organ voluntaries or anthems as about hymns. Hymnology is a subject which shares frontiers with several others — like one of those small counties in England which local government reconstruction has swept away and which, in themselves of limited area, border on several other larger regions. Hymnology has a common boundary with musicology, with literary criticism, with theology and with sociology; it is the study of what people do when for most of the time they hardly know they are doing it, and the application to that study of the principles of larger and more definable disciplines. That sort of activity has been going on for just about a hundred years — not more. These pages are a contribution to it, on the scale, perhaps, of the operations of a specialized ecologist studying an acre or two in what is anyhow quite a small county.

5

I would myself insist that it is a kind of ecology — the study of living things living with each other: of people living with the church and with music and with poetry and with doctrine; primarily, of people and groups of people.

And most of the time wOshall find ourselves looking at the church in times of crisis and of tension. Not that the church has spent much of its time in any other condition — but hymns, we shall find, have flourished most vigorously on the far edges of the church: at what some might call its growing points and others its vulnerable or even heretical points. The pattern forms itself at once: periods when somebody somewhere is tearing up the turf and asking questions and organizing rebellions and reconstructing disciplines produce hymns: when the steam goes out of such movements, or they become part of an expanded main stream, hymn writing goes on in a more tranquil way, but never for very long. Another colour is added to the picture by another 'movement' and that movement brings new hymns and new kinds of hymn into the repertory. That is what we shall be noticing as soon as we start the journey.

II
The First Fifteen Hundred Years

It is everywhere agreed that Christians were singing hymns within a generation of Pentecost. In the short time before anyone achieved the new technique of writing hymns about Christ, Christians sang psalms: for the first Christians were Jewish converts (Acts 2.5) and the psalms were what they knew. But it cannot have been long before they devised ways of singing about the Resurrection and about their Christian experience, and whoever wrote the Letter to the Ephesians, and that version of it which went to Colossae, was aware of this and approved it (Eph. 5.19: Col. 3.16). When John, the exiled minister, wrote to his friends from Patmos in the book we have as *Revelation,* where he punctuates his narrative with snatches of ceremonious poetry (5.13 for example) he may have been quoting what his people already knew, and in any case he was quoting what they would at once recognize as being in a familiar style.

But we have no evidence whatever about how these songs were sung, and the conjecture that on the whole they weren't congregational songs has to be based on the certainty that the congregation had no book to sing from. That there were congregational episodes in them, like the refrains which may have been congregational moments in the Psalms, can be inferred from the fact that in the time of Pliny, man of letters and Governor of Bithynia (Northern Turkey), Christians were *overheard* singing, as he put it, 'Songs to Christ worshiped as God'. That was about 112 A.D. We may confidently suppose, without going further into it, that Christians did have songs at their meetings, and that some of these were simply solos sung by somebody who had just composed them (I Cor. 14.26) and some had refrains which could be joined in. We can be pretty sure that none were continuous congregational pieces such as we know, simply because there would never, at that time, have been multiple copies of hymnals, and people would therefore sing only what they could memorize. Since illiteracy usually goes with good memory they may, in time, have memorized some hymns, but probably these were short pieces, not the elaborate strophic compositions we are accustomed to.

We must suppose, not having any substantial evidence, that these were innocent songs, psalm-like in shape, about what meant most to these primitive Christians — namely, Christ and his Resurrection. (Eph. 5.14: NEB). But another note is heard when we come to the very earliest Christian hymn whose complete text has been preserved. The Hymn *Phos Hilaron* (Cheerful Light) was described by St. Basil, about 370 AD, as 'well known'; it may have been a hundred years old, conceivably two hundred years, in his time. This is a modern translation which preserves the stresses and rhythm of the Greek original:

Christ, gladdening light of holy glory,
glory of God, heavenly Father immortal,
The holy blessed One, our Lord Jesus Christ:

we are now come to the peaceful hour of sunset;
we see the star of evening shine;
we sing to the Father, the Son and the Holy Spirit, one God.

You are worthy at all times to be praised
and honoured with pure and pious songs,
God's only Son, our only life-giver,
wherefore all the world gives glory to you, its Master.*

That is the 'lamplighting hymn': the song associated with the evening service, often held in a windowless cellar or catacomb, where the act of lighting the lamp became symbolic of the Light of Christ entering the world (St. John 1. 5).

And this reminds us that until 313 AD the Church was an illegal institution, subject to suppression as a secret society. Though illegal, and sporadically persecuted, the Church succeeded in witnessing to its faith to such purpose, not only through personal evangelism but through what was for those days an extensive series of important publications, to such good purpose that as soon as it was declared legitimate by Constantine it almost at once was in public business in a big way. Those who prefer to be ironic would say that it had done its work so well during the first three centuries that within a year or two of the official Act of Toleration Christians were fighting one another with zealous ferocity over the right interpretation of doctrine.

Indeed, it is exactly that which forms the pattern of the next episode of in our story. For, apart from two or three ingenious and excellent modern hymns made out of paragraphs in Greek teaching

---

*Various translations of this appear in modern hymnals: that most frequently used begins 'O gladsome light'. This translation is copyright Hope Publishing Co., Carol Stream, Illinois.

books of the first three centuries (I refer especially to the good modern hymns of Francis Bland Tucker, 'Father, we thank thee who hast planted', 'The great creator of the worlds' and 'All praise to thee') and 'O gladsome Light', the first systematic Christian hymnody we have is in the Latin language and comes from the exceedingly troubled fourth century.

The central figure here is Ambrose, c. 340-397, Bishop of Milan. Ambrose was an ecclesiastical statesman whose pastoral genius equalled his organizing ability: the only man alive who was feared and respected by the fierce emperor Theodosius (under whom Christianity became not only tolerated, but the official and compulsory religion of the Roman Empire — from 381 onwards). Ambrose, when he came to the See of Milan, had on his hands a Christendom deeply divided on the subject which is dogmatically organized in our doctrine of the Trinity —specifically, the relation between Jesus Christ and God the Father. There is a reliable tradition that those who were enemies of orthodoxy, the Arians, gave their people songs to sing which would fortify their convictions, and that Ambrose composed songs for Christian orthodox people to sing in reply: from which we at once got the tradition of the metrical doxology. It was good, Ambrose argued, that Christians should sing, but whatever else they sang about, they must sing about the Trinity. And Augustine (354-430) who was rescued back to Christianity from one of the popular imitations by the personal ministry and friendship of Ambrose, tells us quite clearly that Ambrose wanted people to sing.

So this is the first time that the Church gets orders 'from the 'top' to sing hymns congregationally. Modern scholarship attributes only three Latin hymns to Ambrose, and none of them is near the top of modern hymnody. One is that which begins *Deus creator omnium* — a long hymn for an evening service which is mostly a typical evening hymn, praying for protection against enemies mortal and spiritual, and ending with a doxology. Another is 'The eternal gifts of Christ the King', a hymn celebrating martyrdom and reflecting the troubled condition of the church at the time, as well as memories of the Christian martyrs under pagan persecution: that again ends with a doxology.

While a good deal of this is no more than a reliable reconstruction of what happened, and is short of documentary confirmation, it seems likely that Ambrose envisaged a congregational hymnody which would reinforce the faith of Christians under stress. But this is not how things actually turned out. For the Church was having to make another decision of a quite different kind. That was the decision where the centre of tradition should lie. Now that the church was in large public business, and now that it had already become so clear that it was vulnerable to

9

large-scale misinterpretations of the Faith and imitations of it, who was to preserve the tradition that would frame the faith of the people? The answer is inevitable. There must be professional high-grade Christians who were distinguished from the common herd by being literate and learned. Hence the medieval monastic tradition. The story of how this was rescued from a nascent monastic system which was all set to be a museum of eccentricity, individualism and all the qualities of a lunatic fringe is a good story but it must not detain us here. But it was a great contemporary of Ambrose, St. Basil, who rescued it, and from then onwards the great monastic tradition of the middle ages developed, emerging in those huge campuses all over Europe which preserved through the Dark Ages a tradition of culture and literacy as well as the orthodox Christian teaching. There was, in such days, no other way to do it. Christian worship was organized through these institutions: the ordinary lay Christian was content that it should be so.

Such worship, centred of course on the Mass, sustained the faith of the Christian *laos,* and hymnody had no part in it. On the other hand, the daily round of worship in the monasteries themselves (where people *could* read) developed a system of hymns many of which, in translation, are preserved to-day. The earliest of these were hymns, written in imitation of Ambrose in the meter he seems to have invented (four line stanzas, eight syllables each line), or of Pope Gregory I (d. 604), who adapted to hymnody another meter from secular Latin poetry (three lines of eleven syllables and one of five, called 'Sapphic'), simply saying things appropriate to worship at the stated hours of (about) 3 a.m., 6, 9 and noon, 3 pm, 6 and 9. Such hymns as 'Now that the daylight fills the sky' and 'Before the ending of the day' come from this tradition. Later, hymns expressing Christian teaching associated with the seasons, singable to the same tunes, were added, like 'The glory of these forty days' and 'Ye choirs of new Jerusalem', until a complete system of office hymns, as they were called was set up. ('Office hymn' means 'hymn for the routine of the day': a very complete system is in the *English Hymnal,* which can easily be consulted).

None of this was congregational: there wasn't a congregation, in the modern sense. Those present were the members of the campus, or monastery, and they sang the hymns antiphonally to music (plainsong) which is ideally adapted to a community which is constantly, and very frequently, singing together: that plainsong hymnody (not psalmody which is a very different matter) is difficult to adapt to modern conditions of congregational singing is a fact familiar to every choirmaster.

Liturgical developments based on the monasteries gathered two other kinds of hymnody to themselves during the next thousand years.

One was what we might call the liturgical song which was not at first designed to be that, but which was adopted as a fitting adornment to the Offices. This often appears in the form of modern hymns in the metre 8.7.8.7.8.7, like 'Christ is made the sure foundation' and 'Of the Father's love begotten' (which did not originally have the refrain we know). In another metre, 'All glory, laud and honour' is another of these. These came from various origins: 'Of the Father's love' was part of an enormous Latin poem on the subject of the entire Christian Faith by a 4th century poet, Prudentius, who sought to influence intelligent pagans towards taking Christianity seriously. The great *Pange lingua* and *Vexilla Regis* ('Sing, my tongue' and 'The royal banners') were written for a special event — the arrival in France, in the year 574, of relics of the True Cross. Similar special associations are known in connection with other poems, but later the poems were taken into the liturgies of particular days.

The other form of Latin hymn associated with the liturgies is the Sequence: and these, indeed, were in use on special high days in the Mass, being virtually the only hymns that were so used. Their origin is in the Dark Ages, probably the tenth century, in the ingenious answer of local liturgists to complaints from the central authorities about the extravagance of developing music. Extensive melodic flourishes on the last syllable of the liturgical *Alleluia* drew complaints from the Hierarchy, and the answer was to write words under these flourishes which had scriptural relevance to the Feast on which they were sung, thus drawing the fire of the complaints and satisfying the desire of the musicians to mark great days with special musical gestures. These, first known as Tropes ('comments' on the theme of the Feast) became known as Sequences ('what followed the Alleluia') when they became detached, free-standing compositions. A famous example in rhythmical prose is *Victimae Paschali*, from the 12th century, and the best known of all is one of the latest, *Dies Irae*, from the 15th.

Beyond these there are a few Latin poems written without thought of their being sung, and never in fact sung in Latin, which however were turned by translation into English hymns, such as the originals of 'Jesus, the very thought of thee' and of 'Jerusalem, the golden'.

None of this, even when it was sung in its Latin original form, was congregational hymnody. It is safe to say that there was in the middle ages no congregational singing inside church, if by congregational singing we mean singing by the laity. Religious songs there indeed were, but these were communally sung outside church, in association with those semi-secular celebrations of basically religious festivals which formed so prominent a feature of medieval life. Out of these religious ballads and dances came the tradition of the carol, which is always a sociable, legendary, narrative song, usually with a chorus for everybody to join in, and originally associated with a dance.

We have, then, almost nothing from the Middle Ages which had the nature of what we now call hymnody. True, some magnificent examples of modern hymnody are translations of these liturgical or non-liturgical Latin hymns into English; and in modern use they go successfully with measured tunes of the modern kind. But whenever they are so used they are adaptations of old material to a use for which it was not originally designed, in response to a demand of which the medieval liturgists were not conscious.

We may, however, notice just one thing about medieval congregational hymnody, or what we now call carols. These, free from certain dogmatic restrictions, could be in the vernacular, or in a mixture of Latin and vernacular known as the macaronic style (like 'In dulci jubilo'); they dealt with the legendary and fanciful ornaments of the Faith — with the Nativity rather than with the ruthlessly historical Passion, with apocryphal accounts of the youth of Christ, with relics of nature-religion surviving in local Christian customs (like 'The Holly and the Ivy'); and carols are always good-natured and convivial songs, having nothing to do with stress and tension. They are the relaxed, not the bracing, songs of the church. But the habit of singing thus outside the liturgy and outside the sacred building made it almost inevitable that if any protest-movement, seriously challenging some aspect of the medieval faith, wished to increase the enthusiasm of its converts by giving them something to sing, it would be these, not the dogmatic and liturgical hymns, that it would imitate. It was indeed so with the *Laudi Spirituali* associated with the enthusiastic movements of the mid-thirteenth century, and with the early ballads and songs of the precursors of the Reformation. If, for example, it was possible for the villagers of Sens, in France, to devise their famous 'Donkey song', to go with an outdoor procession dramatizing the flight of the Holy Family into Egypt it was equally possible for the Flagellants of southern France, in their demonstrations associated with a conviction that the world would end in the year 1260 (Rev. 11.3) to invent processional songs for their own purposes. And, of course, if it was possible for a devout member of a religious community to write a Latin love-song to Christ like the original of 'Jesus, the very thought of thee', so was it possible for an Italian lay-brother to write the original of 'Come down, O love divine'. There was, outside the sanctuary, much freedom for imagination, and enough religious conviction permeating secular life to evoke sacred poetry.

It was even possible for distinguished theologians to write Latin hymns for special occasions, and there are two eminent, though very different, examples of this. Peter Abelard (1079-1142), the philosopher who in the end fell foul of the authorities for his outspoken rationalism, wrote a series of hymns for use in the Convent of which Heloise was abbess: two of these are preserved to us in 'O what their joy and their glory must be' and 'Alone thou goest forth.' St. Thomas Aquinas, (1227-74), about a century and a half later, wrote three hymns for the Mass of Corpus Christi at the express wish of the Pope (Urban IV), which are known in translation as 'Of the glorious Body telling', 'Laud, O Zion, thy salvation', and 'The word of God proceeding forth' (or in other versions), and which are the only hymns apart from the Sequences mentioned above which we know to have been incorporated in the Mass before the Reformation.

How much more hymnody there was in the Middle Ages which modern use has not preserved we cannot, of course, tell. But the whole period from 400 to 1500 AD was a period of imposed tranquillity during which hymnody developed only in order to support and adorn the timeless liturgy of the Church.

The Greek-speaking church has a history and a nature totally different from the western, Latin-speaking Church; it has been spared the storms and controversies that have vexed the history of the west; it has been (as one of its most distinguished twentieth century authorities, Fr. Florovsky, once said in the present writer's presence) a 'philosophical church', as far as possible riding above the tensions of politics and controversies over doctrine. It finally separated itself from the Roman Catholic Church in 1054, but it was, virtually from the beginning of officially tolerated Christianity, a separate culture. Hymnody has never played a conspicuous part in its worship, which was always much more parish-centered and community-centered than was that of the West before the Reformation; and indeed there are only two well known hymns which come from its liturgies — the Easter hymns translated as 'Come, ye faithful, raise the strain' and 'The Day of Resurrection'. But these were indeed liturgical pieces, their originals being sections of long poems, attributed to the 8th century St. John of Damascus, designed for their special Easter celebrations. Other hymns founded on Greek religious poems, and not used as hymns except in translation, turn up now and again, and yet other formed on prayers from Greek liturgies, like 'Let all mortal flesh keep silence'. These are never translated in their original metres, even when the originals are metrical, or sung, as the Latin ones can be, to their original tunes, and it is highly improbable that any of them were sung as congregational songs in their original language.

But, returning to the Latin hymns, the long period of what seems to us now to be a doctrinal stability overriding the tides of political upheaval and cultural change makes it easy to overlook the fact that hymnody did actually have its origin, in Ambrose's time, in ecclesiastical tension. Hymnody seems to have begun as an act of witness against hostile ideologies, even if it went on for so long, and with so few interruptions or protests, as an activity firmly controlled by the needs of a professionally-administered liturgy. To this the Reformation produced a resounding contradiction, and with the Reformation the real story of hymnody as we now understand it begins.

III

The Crisis of Reformation

It is perhaps allowable to repeat here what I have written elsewhere: that the success of any movement in culture or religion requires at least two people: the one who thought of it and the one who made it stick. The crisis we call the Reformation certainly illustrates that. The Reformation had been brewing for at least 150 years before Luther's gesture of 1517; but it had always been a matter of relatively local dissenting groups under charismatic leaders — Wyclif in England in the late 14th century, Huss in Germany a generation later, Savonarola in Spain, and the early anabaptists, for example. It took the peculiar genius of Luther to make the Reformation, if not as majority movement, at least a viable and unignorable movement.

Without going far into the exceedingly complicated history of all this, it will be enough to say that the Reformation is the religious mode of the Renaissance, and that it depends, like that greater upheaval of which it is a part, on a humanistic demand. Behind Luther's ninety-five theses, which are forbidding reading (and were meant to be) there is the simple demand that lay behind the late fourteenth century Lollards in Britain and all the other dissenting gestures: the simple demand that lay Christians be no longer treated by the Church as if they were children. Judging whether this was a legitimate demand, or justly expressed, would involve an examination of history which we cannot here attempt. Fortunately we don't need to, because we are concerned with Luther's effect on hymnody. For Luther, hymnody was a means of allowing the congregation vocally to participate in public worship, and it is easy to see that as a function of the general demand that the laity be no longer regarded as people who must listen silently, either to instruction or to worship.

The bulk of Luther's 37 hymns, written between 1523 and his death in 1546, were destined to be units in the liturgy of the Mass. He was content that it still be the Mass, although he translated it into German and made changes in it to accommodate his theological demands. Certain important moments in the Mass, up to then celebrated by music confined to the choir, must now be the congregation's property. Now the music of the Mass very broadly falls into two categories: the fixed and settled landmarks of the Mass that are unchanging — the Kyrie, Gloria, Credo, Sanctus, Benidictus and Agnus Dei, which are familiar from countless later choral settings, and the psalms, which varied from week to week and season to season. The core of Luther's hymnody consists of hymns substituted for the fixed units, and of metrical psalms corresponding to the psalms used in the Mass. There is, therefore, in his canon a metrical Gloria, 'All glory be to God on high', a metrical Creed, 'In one true God we all believe', and there are congregational settings of the *Sanctus* and *Agnus Dei*. Beyond this he allowed himself some latitude in translating, or re-working, some of the best known medieval Latin hymns. Further to all this, he wrote hymns to illustrate the Catechism which he drew up for the new church, knowing that the church's teaching would be best implanted in young minds if it was reinforced with hymns.

There are a few Luther hymns which fall right outside the liturgy.* These are not without significance, since they contain the two Luther hymns which are best known to people outside the Lutheran Church. One is the very first he wrote, 'A new Song' (1523), which is a ballad celebrating the virtues of two young men who were burned as heretics at Brussels on 1 July 1523. It is less a hymn than a song of protest and defiance. So, of course, is the universally known *Ein Feste Burg* ('A mighty fortress', or in England, 'A safe stronghold'). The other familiar Luther hymn, *Von Himmel hoch* ('From heaven above to earth I come') is a domestic song written for family use at Christmas.

Luther does not attempt to disguise the polemical content of his hymns. It is absent from those which are taken from the medieval system, like the famous *'Christ lag'* ('Christ Jesus lay in death's strong bands'), or the Advent hymn, 'Savior of the Gentiles come'; but not many of the hymns wholly disguise the fact that Luther's church is a fighting church — fighting on two main fronts, the political and the intellectual.

> The prince of darkness grim,
> we tremble not for him:
> his rage we can endure,
> for lo, his doom is sure...

It is not only the devil, but the Roman Pontiff, that Luther had in mind there, in 'A mighty fortress' (1528); 'Lord, keep us stedfast' is even more outspoken (1541):

---

*For the complete Luther hymns, see Volume 53 of *Luther's Works, American edition, 1965, pp 191-390*.

Lord, keep us stedfast in thy Word,
and curb the Turks' and Papists' sword.

On the other hand, the central doctrine of Luther's system — that which he insisted that the late medieval church had obscured — often appears in hymns which seem to start out from other subjects:

> With thee counts nothing but thy grace
>   to cover all our failing.
> The best life cannot win the race,
>   good works are unavailing —

that is from stanza 2 of his 130th Psalm, and this is from his 12th:

> They teach a cunning false and fine,
>   in their own wits they found it;
> their heart in one doth not combine,
>   upon God's word well grounded.
> One chooses this, the other that;
> endless division they are at,
>   and yet they keep smooth faces.

Luther's vision was of a small collection of hymns, canticles and metrical psalms which, either integrated with the liturgy or at least constantly repeated from month to month through the year would carry the Reformed Faith, through congregatinal singing, into the hearts and minds of the new kind of Christian. We are not yet, and shall not be for a century or two, at the stage where a Christian group has a hymnal of several hundred to choose from. 'You shall have hymns,' Luther seems to have said, 'but I shall decide which they shall be, and they shall be *these*'. His 37 texts were to become a 'canon' hardly less fixed and stable than that of the Bible. Hardly any texts by other writers were recognized by him — and of course his monopoly was easy to establish because there was nobody to touch him in all Germany as a writer. His German Bible is the foundation of the modern German language; in his tracts and commentaries — enough writing to fill 56 volumes in the modern Standard Edition — he was articulate and energetic, and used words the way other leaders used armies.

Modern Lutherans in America — the most active Lutheran communion that does not use the German language — sing seventeen of his hymns. Almost everybody else in the non-Catholic churches outside Germany knows about four or five. Only 'A mighty fortress' is in any sense a popular hymn — and even that is truer in America than in

Britain. The reason for this is not so much doctrinal as practical. The greater part of Luther's hymns are written in long and shapely stanzas (his favourite metre is 8.7.8.7.88.7, and many of his stanzas are longer than that), and the tunes he devised himself or caused others to write are based on the music which was familiar to those people at whom he was particularly aiming — namely, the most alert, intelligent and influential in his country. Certain slanders aimed at Luther have some truth in them, but none have less than the rumour that he adapted 'popular music' for use with his hymns. He wrote his texts on the outward form of the ballads and art-songs which appealed to the top layers of society —the liveliest and most ingenious, not the easiest and most elementary, music of his time. The stanza form of 'A mighty fortress' is typical —nine lines of three different lengths; the tune itself is typical too — a tramping, rhythmically complicated and entertaining tune wandering this way and that but bound together by the immediate repetition of its first phrase, and by the repetition again of half of it at the end. Very few of his hymns are in the short stanzas of 'From heaven high', or 'Savior of the Gentiles'.

Now look at this: there are two tunes called 'Nun Freut Euch' in modern hymn books; one is the one written in 1524 when that hymn first appeared; the other is an alternative for it that appeared in 1535. Musicians will agree that the first one is exciting and imaginative and everything a musician loves; the other, though venerable, always was a relatively dull tune. But it is the 1535 tune that has gone across the Lutheran frontiers into many books still in use. There are one or two other instances of 'simpler' tunes being demanded during Luther's lifetime for such of his hymns as would be carried better by less complicated music. And this is an early symptom of what was later going to happen to Lutheran hymnody in a big way.

Indeed, during the sixteenth century, as the Lutheran church changed from being an army under a brilliant commander to being an institution settling down for a long life, the tendency was for congregations to look for simpler hymns and a somewhat greater variety of choice. The 'grand style' of Luther tended to become petrified into a venerable but slightly impractical form of hymnody: the pieces which, being integral to the Mass, were performed every Sunday survived better than those which were attempted more occasionally. But towards the end of the century the 'grand style' was revived — not only with magnificent literary and musical efect, but in a form which proved to have more staying power than almost any of Luther's own pieces. We refer, of course, to the two great hymns of Philip Nicolai, 'Sleepers, wake' and 'How brightly gleams the morning star'. Here we have stanzas as spacious as any that Luther wrote, with tunes which, although in the later careless ages they disappeared from common use, have never failed to appeal to composers, and have now returned to a place they thoroughly deserve in popular esteem. But these two, composed under great personal stress in 1597 by an otherwise obscure Lutheran country pastor, are the last flowering of the authentic Luther style.

It is very probable that the demand for something simpler and less august than the vintage Lutheran chorale came because Luther's heirs overheard other forms of Reformation hymnody that were being sung with gusto by the anabaptist sects. These — if we may generalize without unfairness — were the more plebeian form of Reformation culture; these groups were inspired and staffed by people who had an interest in the ordinary and undistinguished laity which Luther never had. Their hymnody tended to be less doctrinal and more openly belligerent than Luther's; the people they catered for were liturgically less conservative than Luther, and therefore they wrote far more hymns to fill the gap left by the dismantling of traditional liturgy. Allied with these groups were the Moravian or Bohemian Brethren, who have left us a few tunes that show a surer touch with the popular mind. The texts tended to drop out of common hymnody because of their attachment to the historical situation of these usually persecuted groups (who did not have the advantage of a Luther to lead them on, and were often so scattered and schismatic that it was easy for the authorities to put them down). But one of their texts is the magnificent Easter hymn, 'Christ the Lord is risen again' (1531), and one of their tunes is 'Mit Freuden Zart', a tune whose essential simplicity, further simplified in 1906 by Vaughan Williams, has made it one of the most popular tunes of our own time in America where it is sung very widely to an attractive hymn, 'Sing praise to God who reigns above.' Already we are seeing the difference between the approach to hymnody of the highly cultivated musician and that of the musician of smaller talent who knows what ordinary people can pick up and remember — and this tension has continued, often very creatively, throughout the story of hymnody.

The other 'learned' Reformation was that of Calvin, associated with Geneva. Nothing could be more different than the temperaments of Calvin and Luther: Luther was a genius at public relations, Calvin an essentially private man; Luther an artist with all the artist's impatience; Calvin a scholar with all the scholar's impatience. Luther fought his way out of the medieval Catholic church: Calvin thought his way out of it. Calvin's Reformation was rigidly based on reason, and his church order rigidly founded in discipline. Calvin completely reconstructed worship, being not drawn to preserve as much of its antique and venerable beauty as Luther was. And although he insisted on congregational singing

—and indeed allowed no other kind of singing in public worship — that singing was restricted to Psalms in metre, and such other Biblical passages as could readily go into metre, such as the Lord's Prayer and the Canticles. So with one hand he gave the congregation not only the opportunity but the duty of singing together, and indeed its voice was the only other voice than his own heard in worship (no choir: no organ: no singing in harmony); but with the other he totally forbade any singing of words that were not Biblical.

He began by writing metrical psalms himself, in partnership with Clement Marot (c. 1497-1544) a court poet who had in 1533 devised a metrical psalm to give his aristocratic audience a change, which he felt to be needed, from the lightweight and someties bawdy songs they were accustomed to hearing in their leisure hours. Marot was a useful poet, with a good command of the graceful French meters, and so, in 1539, Calvin, then (at thirty) the minister of the Reformed Church in Strasbourg, produced a metrical psalter containing eighteen psalms and three canticles, done into metre by Marot and himself, each with its own tune.

The rest of the story, which is set in Geneva after Calvin's return there in 1541 (he stayed there until his death, at 55, in 1564), is mainly musical. To cut short a story at length in *The Music of Christian Hymns,* the Genevan Psalter gradually expanded through various editions until all 150 psalms were completed in 1562. Its musical editor in the two important editions of 1542 and 1551 was Louis Bourgeois, who in adapting or composing new tunes, and often in amending tunes from the old Strasbourg Psalter, showed a quite remarkable sense of what a congregation could manage. The metres of the psalms are varied and beautiful — 150 psalms needed 110 different metres — and often very spacious, making it necessary to have tunes that required a considerable effort of congregational memory. In fact, outside the Genevan tradition, these tunes, superb though they almost all are, are not widely used to-day. Of the 125 tunes set to the Psalms and Canticles, only a handful appear in the hymnals. They are: 'Nunc Dimittis', 'Donne Secours', 'Psalm 42', 'Psalm 68', 'Psalm 86', 'Psalm 118', Psalm 124', Psalm 130', Psalm 134', and 'Commandments'. From that list are omitted a few which appear in certain books but are not much sung. But a glance at only a few of those we have mentioned — a glance even only at the 'Old 100th' ('All people that on earth do dwell') or what we call the 'Old 124th' ('Turn back, O man') indicates the quite unique quality of these timeless and archetypal melodies. Although only a few are in use, the effect of this style — the melody that depends on melody alone, with no harmony to support it, and on congregational practicability since if the congregation didn't sing nobody did, is the fountain-head of modern hymnody for all except the Lutherans.

There is one exception to the proposition that the Genevan tunes are not now much used: that is the Reformed Church in Holland, and its offshoots in America and other lands. There the Genevan tunes, and the psalms in translation where they can be translated, are preserved and loved. But it is interesting to notice that the way the Reformed Church has managed to keep them alive is by printing psalters with the words and melody interlined, so that every syllable of a psalm, no matter how long the psalm is, has a note above it. This eases the strain on the congregation's memory and makes the melodies practicable.

Versions of the Psalter harmonized in four or five parts did appear quite soon: these were designed for use in the home. Calvin was suspicious even of that, and quarreled with Bourgeois on that issue; but the year after his death, Claude Goudimel, editor of the complete 1562 edition, did publish a four-part version of the whole Psalter (1565). This, to be used in homes and not in church, was purely vocal and preserved Calvin's veto on instrumental accompaniment. We are about to see a parallel, and more successful development of the same principle in England.

The Genevan Psalter was never revised after 1562. It remains a monument to all that was best in Calvin's conception of religion. That discipline which could so easily become philistine and repressive, and in the administration of which Calvin was constantly at odds with the elders of his church (who were the civic leaders and politicians of Geneva) emerges in the tunes of Geneva as a shining example of how art, when forced through a narrow channel, gains power. They have in hymnology the place that the sonnets of Shakespeare have in literature.

This was Calvin's Reformation responding to the Renaissance demand for greater congregational and lay responsibility: the freedom you seek you shall have, but only when refined by an overriding sense of direction which the Church shall provide. You might say that Calvin saw the infinite possibilities of degeneracy in these new freedoms; you might even say he saw 'The Old Rugged Cross' coming and did what he could to warn us against it. But he didn't win.

IV

The Crisis of Puritanism

Puritanism is a peculiarly English life-style; exported to America, imitated in Scotland, it is actually the least imitable of all Christian life-styles, and the most vulnerable to perversion. The word 'puritan' was first used, as far as we know, in 1564 as a pejorative nickname for people who took a certain line about the English Reformation, but it is mostly applied to the developed form of this life-style and culture which appeared in England in the seventeenth century, and which, under Oliver Cromwell's Protectorate (1649-58) attempted to impose itself on the nation as a political system. We are about to explain what that has to do with our present story.

The English Reformation was as different from those of Geneva and Wittenberg as those were from each other. In the first place, it was occasioned by the act of a layman, not a minister: the layman was King Henry VIII, who reigned from 1509 to 1547, and who for the first twenty years of his reign was an able ruler and regarded by the Pope as a distinguished Defender of the Faith. (That was a title the Pope gave him, which the English Sovereign still holds). But in 1532 the dispute with the Vatican in the matter of Henry's proposal to divorce his first wife led to a clean break. Henry, you might say, called the Pope's bluff and took England out of the system of the Roman Catholic Church by a stroke of his pen.

Protestantism in England had pre-dated this: but Protestants up to 1532 got short shrift from the King. After 1532 the tables were turned, and the project of establishing an English church, preserving the doctrine but not the disciplines of Rome, had to be set in motion. This included the provision of an English Bible (a gesture for which William Tyndale had been burnt as a heretic in 1523), the construction of an English prayer book (completed in 1549), and the reorientation of the church's life away from the monasteries and towards the parishes (hence the famous Dissolution of the Monasteries).

England had been waiting for this since the days of Wyclif — which were 150 years before. But, like the other Reformations, it could not be put into action without the invention of printing: although, unlike those others, it had from the first royal power behind it. So, like the other Reformations, one aspect of it was a response to the congregation's demand, or supposed, demand, to sing.

But here we are in Luther's situation rather than Calvin's; for the new liturgies of the English Prayer Book were adaptations of the Roman rites for parish use, and they retained the essentially conversational character of the old rites: so the congregational demand was largely deemed to be satisfied by their being provided with the responses that up to then had been the business of a monks' choir; and by the encouragement of the congregation to join in, as best it could, with the appointed psalms and canticles. Henry's editors did not attempt to substitute hymns (as Luther had done) for the Canticles and the climactic songs of the Mass: it was enough to translate these into English prose. (And to this day the congregational singing of that admirable but uneven lyric, the *Te Deum,* has been a major problem). The Prayer Book of 1549 provided for only one hymn, to be sung at ordinations, a rather wooden Common Meter version of *Veni Creator,* which has now passed out of use. (The 1662 Prayer Book provided an alternative version of this, almost certainly for responsive reading, which is still known as 'Come, Holy Ghost, our souls inspire.')

Hymnody might never have come to England but for the conjunction of several accidents. It was Thomas Sternhold (d. 1549) who first conceived the idea of English metrical psalms — and this for exactly the same reasons that had caused the French Marot to begin producing his. Sternhold was — yes — a puritan who held the office of Groom of the Royal Wardrobe to Henry VIII's successor, King Edward VI. The new king was eleven when he came to the throne, somewhat sickly in both body and mind: he lived only six more years, and Sternhold seems to have been a tutor and personal adviser to the King, and to have had oversight of court entertainments. The court music of England seems to have been much like that of France, but probably of a ruder and simpler sort. Most popular were the Ballads, in which art form England and Scotland were pre-eminent in the fifteenth and sixteenth centuries. Ballads are stories, historic or apocryphal, set to music, and they had already settled down into their own meter, which was this:

The King sate in Dunfermline towne, drinking his blude-red wine.

That is recognizable as a single phrase of what we in hymnology call Common Meter. Sternhold took up the task of setting the Psalms in meter of this kind, so that they could be sung to the ballad tunes.* He

---

*We have no idea what these tunes were, but the kind of tune ballads were associated with is preserved through the folk-song revival which has given us, in hymnals, tunes like FOREST GREEN.

probably did this during the last two years of his life, and at his death had completed 37. The task was later completed by a team led by one John Hopkins, and the complete Psalter, officially called the *Whole Booke of Psalmes,* but known to the trade as 'Sternhold and Hopkins' or simply 'The Old Version', appeared in 1562, the same year in which the Genevan Psalter was completed.

The official church use of these psalms was at the end of the Office of Morning or Evening Prayer: that is, they were treated (as in Geneva) as hymns, not substituted for the psalms of the day in the liturgy. There are no direct references to their use in the royal Injunctions of 1559, which are the oldest source for directions about what went on in church, unless as some think a stray reference to 'a modest and distinct Song' indicates their authorization. But the title-pages of all the early editions of the Old Version (which became a best-seller and remained one for 250 years) indicate that church use was not their primary purpose. They were really aimed at the homes, where, in literate society, people sang together the way that nowadays (where family life survives) they play cards or other games. It was the puritan mind of Sternhold, shared by the other editors of the psalms, which was sensitive to the social effects of what was thought to be unedifying secular lyric. The puritan mind was morally as well as intellectually fastidious and was peculiarly apt to exalt the virtues of family life.

But there was a strange interruption in this project. The ailing Edward VI was succeeded by Queen Mary, who was a devout Roman Catholic, and who from the beginning of her reign (1553) to its end five years later sought to reverse all that had been done to establish a reformed English Church. How it would have been had she survivied beyond 1558, we cannot tell: had she lived to be seventy and reigned for 45 years as did her successor, Elizabeth I, the Reformation in England might have died. But as it was, distinguished leaders of the English Reformation who were unable or unwilling to face the perils of the new regime left the country, and a number of them settled at Geneva, where they had in use the 1551 (the best) edition of their Psalter; and at once they saw the possibilities of metrical psalmody. They were content to follow Calvin's line, that public song in church should be confined to psalms and metrical canticles, and after a false start or two they devised a kind of music, based on the Genevan style, that would carry their kind of metrical psalm.

Of course it had to be very different music, because they started out with only one metre, and in their complete edition used only a handful. So the Genevan kind of spacious tune had to be crushed into the foursquare and symmetrical ballad metre. What the Genevan editors achieved so brilliantly in a stanza of perhaps eighty syllables the English editors had to cram into fifty-six, all of equal lines, and before long, into twenty-eight, the Common Metre we know. They found themselves quite unequal to the task of providing every psalm with its own tune — had they attempted this, the monotony of meter would have made the tunes sound all much the same. And when they returned to England in 1558 bringing with them an experimental psalter with music (the Anglo-Genevan Psalter, second edition, meaning 'The English Psalter in the Genevan style') they brought only a few tunes, almost none of which have survived in common use. By 1700 the Old Version provided, after input from 150 years of composing, 17 tunes for the canticles and special hymns (more or less one for each) and 39 tunes for the Psalms.

It was different in Scotland so far as church use went. Here, with a Presbyterian order of service in which there was no appointed place for daily psalms and authorized canticles, the metrical psalms were their hymns for the first; and in the titles of all the Scottish Psalters from the first, of 1564, onwards, the church has a more prominent place than in Sternhold. But the musical situation was the same: some adapted Genevan tunes were brought over, but these again have tended to appear in modern books only as period pieces, and to make their way with difficulty into congregational affections.

It was a typically British compromise that saved the psalm tunes from becoming museum pieces. British stuffiness about music tended to make congregations impatient of tunes which set a whole stanza of Ballad Metre (what we call Common Meter Double, CMD), and near the end of the sixteenth century they were finding tunes of half that length quite acceptable. There were one or two of these from the very beginning, but they became much more popular in the 1590s, and it is these that provide some of the best congregational fare in modern books. Few books to-day omit 'Winchester Old' or 'Windsor' from England, or 'Dundee' from Scotland. Many other English and Scottish Psalm tunes in Common Meter from the period 1562-1677 are well known in Britain, though America has tended to be shy of them.

During the seventeenth century, when puritan opinion increased in acceptance in England, many other metrical psalters were produced to compete with the 'official' Old Version, particularly for non-anglican bodies, whose existence, technically illegal up to 1689, was tolerated during the middle years of the century and positively encouraged during the Protectorate. Sternhold and Hopkins's Psalter was on the whole a literary calamity. The one real piece of literature in it is 'All people that on earth do dwell', translated by William Kethe about 1560 from the French of Theodore Beza, to carry the tune from Geneva that everybody knows. Beyond that, virtually nothing survives now. The Scottish Psalter (1564, finally revised 1650 as we know it) was on a different footing, since the Scottish Psalms from the first became the folk-songs of the Scottish people, being, as we said, so much less restricted than the English ones in congregational use. So nowadays we all know one or two of them; but it is the ecumenical movement that has done that. Few people now realize that 'The Lord's my Shepherd' was not regarded as a hymn every editor must include before 1947, when, having been reserved to Scotland ever since 1650, it was catapulted, with an attractive but quite unhistorical tune, into everybody's consciousness at the wedding of the present English Queen Elizabeth II, who is by ancestry half Scots. In this, now a universal religious folk song, we overlook its grammatical infelicities, ('...the quiet waters by') for affection's sake But the Scottish Psalter, inviolable though it is for Scots, is from a literary point of view not much improvement on Sternhold.

But this is an aspect of puritan pressure. Puritan fastidiousness about being precise, combined with a quite new attitude to Scripture once vernacular bibles were in currency, insisted that the only deviations from the Bible text permissible were those required to get the words into metre. *Beauty* was no concern of theirs at all. You must, as far as possible, and indeed at the expense of any kind of elegance, sing 'what the Bible says'. And 'what the Bible says' is, for these people, what the King James Translation causes it to say. 'What the Bible says' is taken straight off the top: no interpretation, no criticism, no overtones, no typology: no notice taken of what was appropriate to the Psalmist and isn't appropriate for Christians. Just 'what the Bible says.'

Look at what is happening. The Reformation is a gesture for human rights, the right to have a personal religion, the right to think: it was set in motion by people of massive intellect, and people of fervent principle concerning the rights of ordinary Christians to more religious judgment than the late medieval Catholic Church allowed them. So — in our particular case — these freedom-fighters of the mind translated the Bible into English for people to read. Indeed they translated it in 1611 (the King James Version) with closer attention to what they could comprehend of the original meaning than any translation up to them had been able to compass. But there it stopped. You have your Bible now: and you must sing it exactly as it is. What criticism, what decision between this and than meaning, was permissible the experts had undertaken, and from here on you follow the experts. It was, obviously, in order for critics of the Reformation to describe the Reformation's leaders as people who had claimed freedom for themselves without ever intending that it should be passed on to their disciples.

It can't be otherwise when you are at war. A freedom-fighting army must have discipline in its ranks. It is only in the twentieth century what Christians of different traditions have been asking whether there can be difference of view without 'war' — and that is what the Ecumenical

Movement is all about. If it lurches and staggers sometimes towards the old conformity and sometimes towards an alarming permissiveness of doctrine, it has at least that to be said for it: and this state of things makes it more difficult to imagine what it was like being a Christian who, whichever side he was on, thought of war as a natural state to be in, and of himself as engaged in it for the highest possible purposes.

But precisely because this was a Christian situation, this didn't work. No attempt to impose an orthodoxy on Christian singers has ever worked. Specifically, the puritan mind which venerated the text of Scripture was capable of criticizing it: and after Britain had been tied down to metrical psalms for 150 years, a critic raised his voice.

Before we name him, however, we will look back for a moment and remind ourselves of the astounding incongruity between the literary quality of the metrical psalms and the musical quality of tunes they were sung to. It's a truism to say that considered as hymn music, as Christian folk song, the finest of the 16th and 17th century psalm tunes are matchless in their quality — their energy, directness, imaginativeness and economy. Almost certainly as actually sung they didn't sound impressive. People certainly didn't sing, as we should say, *well*. Taking trouble to make good music was not in the puritan program for public worship, however much they approved of it in private. But there the tunes are — and if to-day there is no more edifying musical experience in church than to hear a congregation singing 'Let the saints on earth in concert sing' to the tune 'Dundee', and if that rousing experience is partly generated by a quite new tradition of good rhythmic singing and a tradition of organ accompaniment quite unknown to the Scots of 1615, then we have here a good example of the adage in Hebrews, 'that they without us should not be made perfect'; the foundations of good modern hymn singing were indeed laid in the 16th century even if what then passed for hymn singing would be, were we able to hear it, a fairly mournful sound.

We will leave that thought to simmer for a while. Our immediate concern now is with the liberator of English hymnody, Isaac Watts (1674-1748). Watts was a puritan — a puritan to the backbone, intellectually alert, temperamentally cautious and reserved, a nose-in-the-book youngster quite at home in the family of a Congregationalist elder. A puritan asks questions, and in doing so arouses discomfort in the puritan next above him who wants questions asked only by his peers and hopes those below will accept the answers. The question was: why, if Christians sing in church, should they not sing about what means most to them: their Saviour Jesus Christ? The Psalms take us a long way, but not that far. A subsidiary question was, 'Why, if we sing metrical psalms, must they be such sorry doggerel?' In fact — was the King James Version in metre the only possibility for public praise?

The result was 'When I survey the wondrous cross': That answered the first question. And 'Jesus shall reign' answered the second. On the one hand, Watts reasoned, since the Scriptures say all we need to know about Christ, why not devise hymns based on what they say? On the other — since the Psalms themselves mean most to Christians when they reach forward towards the Christian dispensation, why not apply to Christ those royal adulations the Psalmist was content to apply to David, or Solomon, or whoever it was? On this last point he wrote a long and thoroughly trenchant preface (to his *Psalms of David Imitated in the Language of the New Testament,* 1719, and note the title) pointing out the incongruity of putting in the mouths of most Christians the thoughts that occurred to a poet who was a King, and a semitic King at that. So Psalm 72, 'His kingdom shall extend from sea to sea' becomes 'Jesus shall reign. . . .'

But the hymns came first. Between about 1690 and 1707 he wrote well over a hundred Christian hymns, and in his 1709 edition of *Hymns and Spiritual Songs* he had extended this to 360. He began by having his Bible open before him and versifying New Testament passages; he went on to write more imaginative pieces, following thoughts aroused by Biblical texts. Three hundred and sixty hymns in less than twenty years, all done before he was 35, implies swift working, and if you persevere through the complete work you encounter plenty of evidence that he was a hasty writer: sometimes he repeats himself, often he produces rough lines and odd expressions not all of which are of the kind that wouldn't have sounded odd in his time. But you encounter masterpieces too. At his best he becomes the ideal folk-song writer: expressing memorably the thoughts which Christians wish they could express but have always felt. 'When I survey' shows his puritan precision and fastidiousness with words, along with a tenderness and imaginative outreach which are the poet's true gift. Think of him in the act of writing this:

When I survey the wondrous cross
  where the young prince of glory died,
my richest gain I count but loss
  and pour contempt on all my pride.

Forbid it, Lord that I should boast
  save in the death of Christ my God;
all the vain things that charm me most,
  I sacrifice them to his blood.

See from his head, his hands, his feet
  sorrow and love flow mingled down;
did e'er such love and sorrow meet,
  or thorns compose so rich a crown?

29

His dying crimson, like a robe,
   spreads o'er his body on the Tree;
then am I dead to all the globe,
   and all the globe is dead to me.

Were the whole realm of nature mine,
   that were a present far too small;
love so amazing, so divine
   demands my soul, my life, my all.

He himself altered the second line at an early stage — a shade too intimate for folk-song? Or was somebody afraid it might be interpreted as a reference to a certain 'young prince' who, in the Catholic interest, was pretending to the English throne? Modern custom omits stanza 4, and sometimes says 'offering' instead of 'present' in stanza 5. That happens when the 'folk' get their hands on hymns — sometimes they are right, sometimes insensitively wrong.

But there is Watts, with his Bible open at Galatians 6.14, letting his thoughts run free. 'God forbid that I should glory, save in the cross....' — what happens, he says, if you really mean that? Can we bring our congregation to a pitch of devotion, associated with that text, that only poetry can invite them to? 'Pour contempt...', 'all the vain things', 'sorrow and love... love and sorrow', 'love so amazing....' — Watts was no *great* poet; he was just poet enough to invite us to take those few steps that would give us this view.

Imagination — that was what the older puritans had been afraid of. Imagination could do dangerous things with undisciplined minds. But, said Watts, with our hour-long sermons we discipline them enough: it's safe to allow this much imagination. And imagination calls to imagination; people who sing this will start imagining themselves. Very well: if they're my congregation (and of course they were: this is why so many hymns are written by ministers and priests) they'll be safe. Watts felt that doctrine and scripture would keep them safe.

But of course, once you start applying imagination to the Psalms — which he did as soon as he had done with the hymns — then you get not only 'Jesus shall reign' but 'Our God, our help in ages past.' That hymn, nine stanzas as he wrote it, represents five stanzas of Psalm 90. Some of it is meditation on the Scripture' none of it is 'transliteration'. 'Our God....' (Oh, BAD John Wesley to reduce that to the cold 'O God...'!) *'Our* God...' 'Lord, thou has been *our* refuge....' 'From everlasting, thou art God. .' — a clashing collision of tenses to express the timelessness of the God who, being 'from endless years the same', can be 'our guard while troubles last' as well as 'our eternal home.'

No hymnal is without something of Watts; a reader will still find the best working selection of his hymns in *Congregational Praise;* American hymnals are less generous to him nowadays, and in these you tend to find a few of his psalms and only a small handfull of his hymns; the most hospitable is the *Methodist Hymnal* (1966). He is full of doctrinal protein, and very rarely provides much aesthetic carbohydrate.

As we have recently said, it isn't the first, but the best known advocate of a movement whose name is most closely associated with it. A Baptist, Benjamin Keach, had written some communion hymns in 1673, and a puritan poet, George Wither, had written a number of hymns as far back as 1623: but it was Watts who broke the log-jam and caused the logs to come tumbling down the river. Congregational hymn singing was now definitely in business in England.

V

The Crisis of Evangelicalism

Theological upheavals in the church produce predictable crises; and the Reformation was such a crisis; so, within it, was the puritan movement. Evangelicalism, however, emerges first from a quite different kind of crisis, theologically, though not politicaly, unpredictable, a crisis of continent-wide calamity and suffering.

We are here back in Germany, so far as hymns go, but the appearance during the 17th century of *pietism* had an effect on hymnody which has never been questioned or counteracted.

Historically it is simple enough. The Thirty Years' War, 1618-1648, which involved most of the European countries in one way or another, was the most traumatic disturbance of the kind before World War I; it accumulated a prodigious mountain of pure human suffering and misery, and it was by far the most cynical and immoral conflict that history had known up to then. When a continent finds that communications break down, plague devastates large areas, famine disrupts countless lives, and politics become incomprehensible to any but the leaders who go into conflict with both eyes on territorial gain and neither on justice, the most important casualty is organization. Any who hoped to impose religious conformity on large populations, whether Catholic or Protestant, found that the network through which it could be imposed had been broken up into fragments.

Now both the Catholic Church and the Protestant churches had built up administrative networks; the Catholics assumed that the old network of obedience and international conformity was still there; the Protestants, in their new Confessions of Faith and directories of worship set up their own. The assumption was that you, the ordinary lay Christian, did what you were told and believed what you were told to believe by the Augsburg Confession or the Helvetic Confessions; nothing much else seemed to be practicable. Catholics made considerable adjustment to their ancient customs in the light of the Counter Reformation associated with the Council of Trent, which sat from 1545 to 1563. And the new Protestant Church of England had its network fully established by 1570.

The existence of these networks is attested by the precautions built into each of them against dissent, which were often emphatic. If you're a Lutheran or a Calvinist, you do this and this, and you do not do that and that: and you are in trouble if you transgress.

Now it is inconceivable — and history in any case forbids us to claim — that there was no sort of dissent. Within the Catholic church it was still less likely — because of the curious blend of elasticity and authority which that Church always succeeded in achieving — than among the new Protestants. But the chief dissent will always have been among those who said, 'But *this* isn't what the Reformation was about.' As soon as there was a Reformation at all, certain continental groups, usually brought under the general name of Anabaptists, dissented against the 'network' pattern of the large bodies, and the English church history of the mid-16th century contains several groups which certainly dissented. In England there were those who objected to the King's position as supreme governor of the church and said that the government should be in the hands of the church's ministers: these were Presbyterians; and against these there dissented in turn those who thought every local church should be a sovereign body under the government of its own covenanted members — these were, first the Brownists, and later the Congregationalists (with the Baptists, dissenting on a doctrinal issue, taking the same political stand).

The basic question is — how individual can anybody allow the Reformation demand to be? If Luther pivoted the whole thing on 'justification by faith', it was easy for some people to say, 'I will not have my faith dictated to me by anybody but myself and my closest friends.' This is expressed in that famous line of John Milton — a learned first-generation Congregationalist —

New Presbyter is but old Priest writ large.

In other words, we've fallen out of the frying pan into the fire; what we now have is much the same as what we thought we'd escaped from (indeed, rather worse because the Catholics knew a good deal more about administration than these new fanatics do).

It is that cast of mind which comes to the rescue, and indeed celebrates its own liberation, when networks crumble under large-scale calamity. Exactly that is what happened during the Thirty Years' War. Even the newly-reformed Catholic Church was not immune from it, but the Protestants were not slow to grasp the advantages of individual religion over network religion. They found that what they needed was a religious life which did not depend on obedience to a distant authority but was as accessible as a well in the garden would be when the main water supply failed. This, of course, is the religion of personal experience and personal testimony, which we now call evangelicalism.

Pietism, however, is not a contradiction of the structural basis of the Reformation. The word was not used until well after the Peace of Westphalia ended the Thirty Years' War, and when it was used it described a quite new kind of network; it was the progenitor of all these interdenominational networks which, without attempting to loosen people's formal allegiance to this body or that, put in touch with one another Christians of like mind. Pietism gathered all those, of whatever denomination (Catholics included) who sought to live by a religion that depended on no external authority but consisted of regular prayer, works of charity, and the sharing of religious experience. It is essentially a faith which works in small groups or chapters, regarding such chapters as a vital force in revitalizing the formally organized churches. We are familiar with all that in the 20th century. But, although it was 1670 before this network was set up and got the current flowing, the experience out of which it came was fifty years older; for in a situation such as that in which the towns and villages of Europe found themselves during the war, what other religion could sustain the people? Never mind checking for orthodoxy — does our religion help us through this fearful day, this week? That was the question that had to be answered.

The Reformation demand, of course, reinforced the answer. Yes, it is your personal faith which justifies you, and yes, if we are pressed we must admit that the administrative and dogmatic network are secondary to that. Mind you, Luther would have gone on to say, if your personal religion really cuts itself off from the doctrinal sources of scripture and creed, and simply becomes what you personally find it convenient to believe, your private well will do you no good at all because it will be polluted. (The main supply does take some precautions against pollution). Amen, Calvin would have said. But if Luther drove a sharp tool through the notion that the universal church and the universal priesthood were essential to faith, he had only himself to blame if people took hold of that stick by the other end and said they didn't need them at all.

The hymnody of pietism therefore majors in solo religion. Much of it is magnificent, of course, and none the worse for universalizing sentiments that originate in a single human experience. The Psalmist did that. So we have, among hymns that most people know, 'Praise to the Lord, the Almighty', 'If thou but suffer God to guide thee', and 'O Love, who formedst me to wear the image of thy Godhead here', the first of which is by a Reformed Christian, the second by a Lutheran, the third by a Catholic. 'Now thank we all our God' is one of the very few hymns from the German 17th century that we are not in the first person singular: and that was a table grace for a family before it became a majestic universal hymn. The greatest writer of hymns in this style was

Paulus Gerhardt (1607-76), who wrote 123 hymns of which many are known outside Germany: among them are 'O sacred head', 'All my heart this night rejoices', and the original of 'Commit thou all thy griefs' (known sometimes by the opening of a later verse, 'Give to the winds thy fears'). These, helped on by the superb music of Johann Crüger (1596-1662), were the foundation of evangelical hymnody, — free ranging, poetically imaginative, and intensely personal; different in all these ways from the hymns of Luther and the Psalms of Calvin.

And all this hymnody was in its nature either family hymnody or solo hymnody rather than congregational song. Although a number of the tunes associated with these hymns are now in the common stock —and we refer here to any German hymn tune written between about 1620 and 1720 — they were designed to be solos. Among the huge number that have disappeared into museums you will find many which are congregationally impracticable — having vocal colaratura passages, wide compasses (high G is not uncommon) and all the other attributes of solo vocal music in the first decades of the operatic style. Just as the 23rd Psalm, a solo or even a soliloquy, is central to the common devotion of Christians, so is a hymn like 'Deck thyself, my soul' *(Schmücke dich)*) one of the very first Eucharistic hymns to be written in the first person singular; and just as the ecstasy of Psalm 40 transcends its intimate personal language, so, for many generations, has that of 'Fairest Lord Jesus.'

But perhaps it is already clear that religion was moving into difficult and risky country. For what happens when a religious life-style appropriate to a solitary person or to a group of friends who know one another very well expands over large numbers of people and builds up a tangible, palpable network on the pattern of the networks it began by rejecting? The answer is, in the case of German pietism, the Count Nicolas von Zinzendorf.

Zinzendorf (1700-60) was the founding father of modern Moravianism, and among other activities we are about to examine wrote a very large number of hymns — some say, over 2,000 — of which the most familiar now is 'Jesus, still lead on'. I am about to quote from the book *Enthusiasm,* by Ronald A. Knox (1950), which relies for its data on Frey's *True and Authentic Account* (of the Moravians), Holmes's *History of the Protestant Church of the United Brethren,* and Hutton's *History of the Moravian Church.* These are all primary sources, and it is as well to tell the reader that, in view of what follows.

...Zinzendorf was a German aristocrat; the blood of landowners ran in his veins. It is not surprising, therefore, that at the age of twenty-two... he bought an estate at Bethelsdorf in Saxony, installed his friend Rothe as pastor, and settled down to make a model village of it, to his own spiritual specifications. You see in him the forerunner of those Victorian county magnates who provided so many English villages with a church and a clergyman precisely of their own colour, and sought, with varying success, to woo the religious sympathies of the tenants... 'The Count's family pew in the church was a small gallery or raised box over the vestry; the box had a trap-door in the floor; the pastor, according to the Lutheran custom, retired to the vestry at certain points in the service; and the Count, by opening the aforesaid door, could communicate his wishes to the pastor.' [Holmes] I hope it is not flippant to see, in that admirably arranged trap-door, a symbol of Zinzendorf's whole ecclesiastical method. For the remaining thirty-eight years of his life he was, to all intents and purposes, the Pope of a world-wide organization; under a bewildering variety of titles he had the last word in everything.

(Knox, p. 400)

It is more pertinent, in discussing a man who was so very much the ecclesiastic, to examine his public quantities. 'He was not always strictly truthful;...' [Hutton]. A more noticeable trick about the man was a kind of ostentation which led to recklessness in money matters. He travelled with a secretariat of forty persons, and when he came to London made his headquarters at Lindsey House, Chelsea, which he 'did up' at an expense of £11,000. [Addison, *the Reformed Church of the United Brethren*]. In spite of all his generosity to it, the church which he had created found itself, a few years after he died, £150,000 in debt. [Holmes]. He was also imperious... 'dominant, not to say domineering, and with a turn for organizing, (his enemies would call it an itch for interference) which insisted on remoulding whatever came to hand.'[Jenks, *The Moravian Brethren in North Wales*].

Knox p. 418

That is not gossip; it is a judgment extracted from the writings of several historians sympathetic to the Moravians. The career of Zinzendorf is an object lesson, which nobody nowadays cares to attend to, in the consequences of allowing personal religion to become detached from objective doctrine. The way is left clear for the religious dictator, whose pattern of operation is faithfully laid down by Zinzendorf; for what he believed he was founding was a spiritual network, by relation to which all the established churches should find the way to unity. His personal arrogance and intolerance, which not everybody discerned behind his energy and freedom in spending money, ensured that after his death Moravianism almost disappeared; indeed its survival in a church body which today, especially in the United States, manifests plenty of vigour and maintains a distinctive character, is the triumph which all those historians are at pains to celebrate.

The unfortunate chaplain to this outfit at Bethelsdorf was J.A. Rothe, who was among the Moravian hymn writers whose work appealed especially to John Wesley; and a hymn known to some Methodists. 'Now have I found the ground' is typical of his work. The English version is Wesley's, and it is a fine piece, even if its ecstatic mixing of metaphors becomes somewhat daunting.

It is, indeed, Moravian hymnody that provides the first link between German and the later English evangelicalism. Neither in the hymns of Zinzendorf nor in those of his followers do we find any hint of the dangers latent in anarchic evangelicalism — except in this: that they continue to be, as were all the pietist hymns, *solos*. Nothing could, perhaps, be more edifying than to think of, say, the original of 'All my hope on God is founded', or 'O God, my faithful God' being sung as a solo in a home or a small meeting: the solo performances of Chairman Zinzendorf in committee are, we might say, less attractive.

John Wesley has, inevitably, been compared with Zinzendorf. At any rate, Zinzendorf's style appealed to him. Caught at a moment when his sense of direction had faded, when he had reason to believe that all his efforts up to the age of 35 to interpret in a manner relevant to his time the dictates of a Christian conscience, his meeting with certain Moravians formed a kind of catalyst which caused what is known as his 'conversion.' Wesley was another born administrator, in the old fashioned sense. He had, uniquely among the numerous progeny of that dedicated Epworth rector, Samuel Wesley senior, a feeling that 'things ought to be changed and could be, given the know-how.' At Oxford, in the secluded environment of a university handily adorned with plenty of people of thoroughly secular values, he had tried it; in Savannah, Georgia, he had tried it. Returning across the Atlantic after the rather lame conclusion of a mission he later referred to as more or less abortive, he encountered the colourful fervour of Moravian hymnody and theological writing: and he saw, in 1738, the Bethelsdorf experiment in its full flight of efficiency and eloquence.

Perhaps his genius showed itself most in that he was able at once to translate all this into English — as symbolically he translated its hymns. He was not an aristocratic amateur but a well-educated priest of the Church of England with what one can only call the highest professional standards of ministry and religious conduct. He had the magnetism that made disciples, and the lofty temperament that often lost them to the cause; he lived to be not sixty but eighty-seven; and the movement he set going left no part of the public life of England untouched. Once again, he sought to found Methodism, not a Methodist Church. Methodism should be a network of all Christians, of whatever allegiance, who lived by a 'method' — who, spiritually, meant business. The Methodist Church, or more classically Connexion, was founded only after his death.

It was really not much good pursuing parallels between John Wesley and Zinzendorf; what, in Zinzendorf's influence, corresponds to the complete turn-around in religious sense that Wesley created throughout Britian? But one enormously important difference between the two men was that John Wesley had a gifted brother. (Actually he comes of a family which produced geniuses, not least in music but also in many other fields, for another century and a half). John lived from 1703 to 1791: Charles his younger brother, from 1707-1788. Their partnership lasted exactly fifty years, and in it Charles was the hymn writer: indeed, in many other ways he was a steadying influence, and at some times was the only person who could get through to John at all.

Charles wrote religious poems throughout his life — the total count in the authorized edition is 8,989. Many of these are hymns, and many of those hymns are very brief — one or two stanzas only — but it was a notable achievement, especially when we remember that nothing we use as a Charles Wesley hymn was written after 1765.

Enough has been written about this monumental output to save our going into it here at any length. Like Watts, Charles Wesley is in every hymnal: the English Methodist Hymnal (1933) contains 240 of his pieces, and the previous edition of 1904 had 440. No hymn book worth mentioning has fewer than fifteen. Among them, including hymns abridged and altered in modern use, are 'Lo, he comes with clouds descending', 'Hark, the herald angels sing', 'Christ the Lord is risen to-day', 'Hail the day that sees him rise', 'Love divine, all loves excelling', 'Christ whose glory fills the skies', 'Forth in thy name, O Lord, I go' and 'Rejoice, the Lord is King' — to mention only a handful that are in every hymnal worth opening.

What was this extraordinary explosion of hymnody designed to do? It was designed to serve the avowed purposes of the new evangelicalism in England. Now the new evangelicalism was different from pietism in this, that it was a travelling evangelism. It was designed from the first to be centred on small groups of dedicated Christians, called 'classes', but to carry the Gospel into every place which the somnolent churches of early 18th century England had neglected. It was designed to be not only a ministry to the very devout, but a ministry to the lost: to contain not only a discipline but an invitation. The idea of personal power-seeking was never in John Wesley's mind — he simply did not leave himself time to consider it.

None the less, the pietist style of hymnody was just what he could use. The Wesleys decided at once that they needed hymns of colourful fervour that would make their message memorable. For them hymns were not part of a liturgy (or, as the metrical psalms had been, rather awkward adornments of it). They were arrows which would pierce where preaching, even evangelical preaching could not penetrate.

Now Charles was a facile writer, and could produce hymns pretty easily. But unlike the metrical psalmodists, and some of the lesser German pietists, he was profoundly well-read, a professional in the use of language, and a very devout disciple of the church's doctrine, as well as having a complete command of the words of the Bible. So he wrote what John wanted: hymns for the devout in class-meetings, and hymns for the heathen in the fields where their open-air preaching was done. He would write very simply: he could write in remote and complex phrases; he could do something as clear and captivating as the hymn lying behind 'Hark the herald', and something, next day perhaps, as allusive and contemplative as 'Come, O thou Traveller'. But, while many of his hymns make first-rate congregational material, they were mainly solos; certainly those designed for outdoor-work must have been, for the listeners had no books. And the music which went with them, in the first tune books, is always scored as solo songs were scored — with a melody and a figured bass. Even when the words are universal and communal, the music was of the kind inspired by Handel and the lesser opera-composers of the 1730s.

Hardly any of this music is in general use now; one of the very few early tunes written for a Wesley hymn that we still use is by Handel himself, written for 'Rejoice, the Lord is King': and that was, as soon as it was composed, lost to sight for fifty years before it was rediscovered.

The great distinction of Charles Wesley, then, is that, at his best, he combined the intimate with the universal. These qualities will be found in any hymn of his one cares to look up: but consider the extraordinary profundity, the poetic paradoxes, of this:

O come, ye sinners, to your Lord,
in Christ to Paradise restored;
his proffered benefits embrace,
the plenitude of Gospel grace:

a pardon written with his blood,
the favour and the peace of God,
the seeing eye, the feeling sense,
the mystic joys of penitence;

the godly grief, the pleasing smart,
the meltings of a broken heart,
the tears that tell of sins forgiven,
the sighs that waft your souls to heaven;

the guiltless shame, the sweet distress,
the unutterable tenderness,
the genuine, meek humility,
the wonder — why such love to me?

the o'erwhelming power of saving grace,
the sight that veils the seraph's face;
the speechless awe that dares not move,
and all the silent heaven of love.

(Methodist Hymn Book — English — 325)

That, many will say, is 'unsuitable for modern use.' It certainly is very intense, very strange to the modern mood; it wears its heart on its sleeve in the way in which modern hymn writers don't. But let it be remembered — it was not intended, as modern hymns are, for 'congregational singing'. It was a poem either to be sung, like chamber music, by a small group of people who knew each other intimately and shared with each other the secrets of the soul: or perhaps to be sung to a hushed group of people by a soloist. Modern taste may be more civilized; it is undoubtedly coarser. But when we referred a few pages back to the difference between modern congregational singing and what one would have heard in the 17th century we were referring to a kind of activity which as yet was quite unknown in England.

It is because hymn singing now is so different from what either Watts or the Wesleys knew that we now are most familiar with the most 'public' of Wesley's hymns. Actually, the lines just quoted are more typical of Charles Wesley than most of the hymns of his now sung. A look through the English *Methodist Hymn Book* (1933), pausing on the unfamiliar ones, will make that clear at once. At present the Wesley hymns are mostly for reading and meditation and perhaps the occasional solo or choral piece rather than for the congregational singing we are now accustomed to. But that is a point we must take up later when we consider the hymnody of present-day evangelicalism. Meanwhile we can just notice the exquisite sensitiveness and insight which enable him so accurately to portray the silence of heaven, the 'joys' of penitence, and the 'guiltless shame.'

It was two hundred years before Methodism produced a hymn writer worthy to be compared with Charles Wesley, or indeed an important hymn writer at all. His influence was almost a hundred per cent effective in that sense. The only way in which he influenced other writers was to demonstrate that hymn writing of this kind was possible. More — he set a standard of disciplined fervour which many in their different ways in later ages have attempted to make their own. But you cannot lay your finger on any later hymn writer and say that he is a direct disciple of Charles Wesley.

In two other ways, however, Evangelicalism had an important influence on later hymnody. One of these is usually a bad influence. Of Zinzendorf a historian wrote (as we quoted just now) that he moulded whatever came to hand. Not in text writing, since it was all in one pair of hands, but in music, one sees quite early the tendency of evangelicals to 'mould' — to alter what 'comes to hand' so that it conforms to their patterns. It is in tune books associated with the evangelical kind of singing that we first see on a large scale old tunes altered, indeed sometimes totally refashioned, so that they will lose the asperities of old music and conform to the smooth style of contemporary music. We know nowadays how often tunes appear in hymnals in a form quite different from what their composers designed: well, the Wesleys did not quite invent this fashion, but their musicians certainly gave it prestigious approval.

Without being over-technical we can say that something had happened to music analogous to what had happened to theology — though for entirely different reasons which don't concern us. The point is that music, which in the 16th century was assumed to be a communal activity for singers, had become a public activity to which more and more people were *listening*. During the 17th century a style developed, of which the English became generally aware after the Restoration in 1660 of a court which had been exiled to France for eleven years, which was not conversational but rhetorical: very roughly, not performed by several voices singing parts of equal importance, but by, essentially, a single voice singing a melody for which the instruments provided an accompaniment. Although the lute-music of early soloists like Thomas Campian (c. 1613) was music of this kind, it was designed only for intimate groups; the 'new music', as people tended to call it, started off in a direction which produced the virtuoso singer and player. What used to be a 'consort' — people singing for pleasure or for devotion —became a 'concert' — people performing solo or in groups for an *audience*. We said that early Wesley tunes were scored for melody and bass only: that is exactly the effect. Modern ears (of the more innocent kind) still think of music as having a 'tune' which takes precedence over whatever other sounds are being made. Modern music-making includes the star pianist, violinist, or singer, the highly-skilled chamber group, the orchestra, all of whom make music at a standard far beyond what even the musical members of their audiences can hope to reach.

In the 18th century this was new: but its tendency to focus the attention of a crowd upon a soloist, as on a 'tune', coincided exactly with the evangelical tendency to address an audience in a teaching and hortatory tone.

You could say, indeed, that the worship of the 17th century puritans was like chamber music, in that a minister who preached presupposed in his congregation a learning in the scriptures, and a faculty of attention, comparable to the efforts he put into his preaching, and that no puritan meeting house (they called it that) could function without the assumption that responsible churchmanship on the part of all present was to be assumed.

But in Wesley's time there was a huge demand for 'tunes', and an ample reservoir from which to draw them, to be found in the music of the light operas current in Handel's time. The promoters of opera in London in the 1730s more or less invented 'show business' in developing a new faculty for calculating exactly what would draw the people in crowds. The Beggar's Opera, the Cobbler's Opera, and many other attractions of the kind are the real source of early Wesley hymnody. Oddly enough, Handel couldn't make opera pay, and retreated into oratorio. But the new public demand for instant music put pressure on the editors of hymn tune books to recast older music so that it sounded like the instant music people now wanted. The Evangelicals did a great deal of this; and they also, again following the light opera compilers, pressed into service many secular airs and indeed snatches occasionally from the resounding popular Handel oratorios. Singing 'There is a land of pure delight' to the tune of 'Drink to me Only' was a commonplace in the late 18th century — and it certainly was not the sort of behavior the puritans would have countenanced for a moment.

So we have the beginning here of that popular adjustment of ancient tunes to suit contemporary taste which was protested against only in the early 20th century, and of that use of secular music for hymns which again has now mostly passed away. You could call this a debasement of popular taste.

Secondly, however, the modern custom of singing hymns in four-part harmony seems to have begun also with the Evangelicals. Among the widespread philanthropic enterprises inspired by evangelicalism was the foundation of large charity schools, mostly for orphaned and destitute children; and these institutions formed choirs which made a great deal of music. Similar choirs were formed in charity homes for adults in various conditions of misfortune, like the Magdalen Hospital. The new choral technique was applied to hymnody, and a new kind of hymn tune, which often composed hymns into anthems, with different tunes for each stanza, began to appear, which was imitated in the early 19th century when choral singing became generally popular.

But here again, a large demand tended to debase the currency, and after the spirited music of the first generation of Wesley hymns, as found in *Harmonia Sacra* (published in the 1750s) we tend to find a sinking downwards into repetitive platitude, and the propagation in hymnody of 'instant music' to match the urgent needs of the new evangelism.

VI

The Time of Peace and Expansion

And now we come to a time when hymnody began to become self-propagating, without the need of a stimulus from outside. This is the period between about 1775 and 1833. Watts and Wesley had shown that English hymnody was a going concern. The only dissuasives from continuing to nourish it were in the excellence and the prolixity of the work of those two authors. Still, there were people who saw a need for new hymnody, perhaps rather in the style of Watts than in that of Wesley, but designed to nourish those other parts of the church which evangelicalism had awakened. They were not, as we have said, Methodists: they were Baptists or Congregationalists or evangelical anglicans.

There was, for example, the Baptist Robert Robinson, whose haunting and rugged lines beginning 'Come, thou Fount of every blessing' express so faithfully the ecstatic unbalance of his character. There was the anglican Thomas Toplady (1740-78), a compulsive religious journalist and as literal a Calvinist as every lived, who constantly attacked John Wesley, but whose 'Rock of ages' Wesley accepted as one of the few hymns not by himself or his brother in the 1780 *Hymns for the People Called Methodists*. There had been, long before, the Congregationalist Doddridge, an admirer and disciple of Watts, who wrote the original (in our hymnals much altered) of 'O God of Bethel', and the stirring Advent hymn, 'Hark, the glad sound.' He lived from 1702 to 1751 and his more than 300 hymns were collected and published after his death. There was another anglican, Edward Perronet, who wrote 'All hail the power of Jesus' name, a heraldic hymn using the images of the Book of Revelation, which Watts would have been proud to write. There was the evangelical Thomas Olivers who put together the twelve verses of 'The God of Abraham praise' — which in America are mostly now replaced by an American version of the same original, usually beginning with the same words. The Charity foundations produced, anonymously, 'Praise the Lord, ye heavens adore him' just before 1800, and another excellent hymn, not known yet in America, 'Spirit of mercy, truth and love' (Hymns A & M 153) which again recalls Watts's style. There was, in Wales, celebrating the evangelical revival in that country, William Williams who in 1745 wrote the Welsh original of 'Guide me, O thou great Jehovah,' — still (astonishingly when one considers the great outpouring of hymnody in Welsh during the next century) the only Welsh hymn widely sung in English.

But above all there were John Newton and William Cowper. John Newton (1725-1807) was the perpetual curate of Olney — then an obscure village in Buckinghamshire; and William Cowper (1731-1800), the best known English poet of his generation, was his close friend. Here was this dead and gone parish, thrown to Newton like a crust to a dog because his rackety life as a sailor in charge of a slave-ship had made bishops shy of him (he was perpetual curate, not Vicar or Rector, which broadly meant that he did a resident clergyman's work for next to no stipend): and the energetic and dedicated Newton aimed to bring it to life. Part of this project was a weekly prayer meeting at which he needed hymns for the people to sing. Cowper, shy, withdrawn, depressive, but a true poet, was the man to ask to write the hymns; and between about 1772 and 1774 he wrote sixty-eight. Overtaken then by a nervous breakdown, he said he could do no more, and Newton completed the collection with 280 more, making a hymnal of 348 hymns called *Olney Hymns*. Never in the history of hymns was there so felicitous a partnership. Cowper in his hymns brings to the literature a quite new standard of poetic fastidiousness, without ever relaxing the tension of evangelical devotion. So we have perfect things like 'God moves in a mysterious way', 'Sometimes a light surprises' and 'Hark, my soul, it is the Lord,' and 'O for a closer walk.' Too intense, some of them, for modern devotion — but there is never a word misplaced or misused, never a metrical roughness; and there is always something memorable and commanding.

Newton, by contrast, has the familiar evangelical ruggedness; he gave us 'How sweet the name of Jesus sounds', 'Gloroius things of thee are spoken' (sadly mauled in almost all American hymnals) and 'Amazing grace'. Here are two quotations, one from each author, from hymns less often sung now than they used to be, which display their complementary talents. This is Cowper — verses 3 and 4 of 'What various hindrances we meet':

> Restraining prayer, we cease to fight:
> prayer makes the Christian's armour bright;
> and Satan trembles when he sees
> the weakest saint upon his knees.

> While Moses stood with arms spread wide
> success was found on Israel's side;
> but when through weariness they failed,
> that moment Amalek prevailed.

Simple, gentle, biblical: just what was needed for the teaching and building up of those villagers. Here is a characteristic passage from Newton — the opening of his 'Begone, unbelief':

> Begone, unbelief: my Saviour is near,
> and for my relief will surely appear;
> by prayer let me wrestle, and he will perform,
> with Christ in the vessel I smile at the storm.
>
> Though dark be my way, since he is my Guide,
> 'tis mine to obey, 'tis his to provide.
> Though cisterns be broken and creatures all fail
> the word he hath spoken shall surely prevail.

They didn't read much, but they read their Bibles, and they would pick up the allusions to Genesis 32.24, Philippians 1.6, Mark 4.38, Deuteronomy 29.29, Matthew 6.31 and Jeremiah 2.13 (King James, of course) packed into those eight lines. *Olney Hymns* remains, after Watts and Wesley, the richest source of 18th century lyric devotion.

But pause a moment. This is the first time we meet a recognized man of letters as a hymn writer, and the first time we have mentioned a layman writing in English. Cowper, though one of the only two English poets of the first rank who wrote hymns (the other was Robert Bridges whom we shall meet later) was not the first layman in the field. Apart from George Wither, whom we mentioned in passing earlier, the first lay hymn writer was in fact Joseph Addison (1672-1719), who, greatly admiring the then very new work of Watts, himself wrote five hymns. He was at the time editor of the *Spectator,* England's longest-running literary weekly, and in 1712 he published some lines of Watts, following them at two-weekly intervals for ten weeks with hymns of his own. It is a remarkable fact that in current English hymn books all five are still printed; in America we usually confine ourselves to 'The spacious firmament' and 'When all thy mercies.' He does not attempt the lofty scriptural dogmatism of Watts, and of course he never lived to see Wesley's work: his is good layman's writing, exquisitely turned, much more fastidious about words and phrases than Watts, and still valuable.

But Cowper is something else again; and indeed when one examines the flood of evangelical hymnody that was about by the time he started writing hymns (we have mentioned only a handful, and the best of them) we can see that the time was ripe for the civilizing of hymnic language. There was a terrible tendency in the evangelical underworld to slam words down on paper in the conviction that the Christian subject of the hymn would cause everybody to overlook its literary crassness. Somebody who moved in the secular literary world, who knew what good writing was, who developed his craft in the unsheltered workshop of secular letters, was exactly what was wanted.

This, however, could only have happened in what we are calling a 'time of peace', when hymns were written not to celebrate a Reformation or to minister to people in desperate physical need, or even simply as the spinoff from theological controversy, but simply because people wanted hymns. True, the need of Olney was in Newton's eyes critical; but it was local. You might almost say that the talent of Cowper was wasted on Olney — and if it had not been shared by the succeeding ages it almost would have been. But at least now there was time to consider the subtle graces of poetry, and see how they could assist in making the Gospel lyrical.

Another region in which something comparable happened was Scotland. Scotland was not really touched by the evangelical style until the turn of the century — and then, curiously enough, its product was not Scottish Methodism (for Methodism in Scotland remains an English culture) but Scottish Congregationalism of a quite distinctive kind. So the reign of metrical psalmody was supreme in that country —until the question was first asked in 1745 whether other parts of the Bible could not be adapted for congregational singing. The Church of Scotland deliberated this and eventually turned it down, but a generation later the General Assembly authorized an addition to the Psalms of sixty-seven *Paraphrases,* which were passages of scripture from both Testaments rendered into verse with the same care that the metrical psalmodists had shown for the faithful reproduction of Scripture — but with very much greater elegance. Indeed, the paraphrasers (among whom the chief were John Logan and John Morison) used a good deal of Watts and Doddridge (no Wesley) and altered them — quite often for the better. We mentioned 'O God of Bethel' just now. As we have it, it is mostly the work of the Paraphrasers, and the reader may judge the difference in style from the original:

O God of Jacob, by whose hand
   thine Israel still is fed,
who thro' this weary pilgrimage
   hast all our fathers led;
to thee our humble vows we raise,
   to thee address our prayer,
and in thy kind and faithful breast
   deposit all our care.
	O God of Bethel, by whose hand
	   thy people still are fed,
	who through this weary pilgrimage
	   hast all our fathers led;
	our vows, our prayers, we now present
	   before thy throne of grace;
	God of our fathers! be the God
	   of their succeeding race.

Doddridge	Paraphrasers, 1781

Or compare the style of such excellent Paraphrases as 'Come let us to the Lord our God' or 'The race that long in darkness pined' with that of

'The Lord's my Shepherd', and one sees at once that 'style' was now beginning to be a genuine consideration, and fervor was no longer deemed to be an excuse for its neglect. Of course it was to some extent the work of great stylists like Dryden and Pope that made people aware of the pleasures of good writing: and indeed, though neither of those masters wrote a hymn intentionally, both were later admitted gratefully to the hymnals by editors: Dryden with his 'Creator Spirit, by whose aid' and Pope with a sturdy hymn made out of a longer poem, 'Rise, crowned with light', known as yet only in America.

So the scene is set for a two-pronged advance of hymnody consequent on the evangelical awakening. One arm of this advance reached towards a celebration of the new interest in foreign missions.

Evangelical energy could not for long be contained within the British Isles. The needs of the heathen in what we would now call the Third World came before the eyes of certain visionaries, and from 1792 onwards all the main-line denominations founded societies for the pursuit of foreign missions. The next two generations are the heroic missionary period, and their chief singer is the third important layman in our story, James Montgomery (1771-1854). Montgomery was a journalist, of Moravian Scottish stock though later an anglican; he combined a ready talent for writing with a social conscience which was directly inspired by evangelicalism, and in his young days, in the 1790s, worked on, and later edited, a paper in Sheffield, the *Iris,* which was regarded as one of the most radical journals in the country. It campaigned ceaselessly for the abolition of slavery, it praised the French Revolution for its liberation of the poor, it criticized mercilessly all governmental and institutional activities which seemed to it to disregard human rights. It was not of political matters that Montgomery wrote, however, when he wrote hymns. It was, in the first place, of the triumph of missions, and 'Hail to the Lord's Anointed' and 'O Spirit of the living God' are excellent and deservedly popular hymns of his taking this line.

But he was also a stylist. Having found this talent for poetry of the kind that makes good hymns, he turned to writing on all subjects — he had written over 300 by the time he died — and also to editing. Not only did he give us such excellent things as 'Stand up and bless the Lord', 'Lift up your heads, ye gates of brass' and 'God is our strong salvation'; he also 'rescued' a number of hymns by earlier writers for his age by rearranging or re-composing them. Among these, almost certainly, are the admirable Christmas hymn, 'Christians, awake' — indispensable in England through not well known in America, — the charming devotional poem 'O Thou from whom all goodness flows', and a version of 'Jerusalem, my happy home' (often, but wrongly, attributed to a certain

49

Bromehead) which used to be popular before the 16th century original was restored. One may as well notice here that there are a number of hymns we now sing in their original versions which we might never have noticed if past generations had not known them in altered versions and made them popular. We shall return later to that point.

Montgomery was indeed involved in a controversy which had a vital effect on hymnody; this hymnal he edited, or helped to edit, was the eighth edition of a book provided for St. George's (anglican) church in Sheffield by its Vicar, Thomas Cotterill; and when members of his congregation became restive about being obliged to learn so many new hymns, associating hymn singing with a style of religion they did not care for, they dredged up an ancient church law that prohibited the singing in church of hymns 'of human composure' — the same law that tied the church down officially to metrical psalms. In the resulting action in the church courts a law that had for generations been a dead letter in the Church of England was upheld, but the Archbishop of York contrived a way of getting it altered, indeed repealed, and from 1821 hymns were officially legitimate in the Church of England. Cotterill and Montgomery were responsible for that.

An example of Montgomery's style — smooth and at the same time direct — is in one of two hymns he wrote about prayer; this one is 'Prayer is the soul's sincere desire', and these are its third, fourth and fifth stanzas:

Prayer is the simplest form of speech   Prayer is the contrite sinner's voice.
    that infant lips can try,   returning from his ways,
prayer the sublimest strains that reach   while angels in their songs rejoice
    the Majesty on high.   and cry, 'Behold, he prays!'

Prayer is the Christian's vital breath
the Christian's native air;
his watchword at the gates of death:
he enters heaven with prayer.

Montgomery follows Cowper in matching fervor with style. Most of his hymns were written between about 1810 and 1825, though he revised many of them at a later stage. And about that time a response to the Romantic Movement in literature was found in the English writers who turned not only to a new respect for style but to new subjects. And here the Anglicans, newly liberated by the law of 1821, began to challenge the pietists. Could not anglican worship be positively enhanced by hymnody? And if so, should not that hymnody have a touch of elegance, perhaps at the expense of some of those lofty theological visions that the 18th century writers most rejoiced in? In answer to that question we begin to get real poetry. Reginald Heber, Vicar of Hodnet, broke new ground with 'Brightest and best' — a hymn shamelessly addressed not to the Saviour but to a star; and with 'Bread of the world' and 'Holy, Holy, Holy'; Sir Robert Grant replaced the old metrical version of Psalm 104 (a rugged thing, in all conscience), with 'O worship the King', and Henry Francis Lyte, another anglican incumbent of a tiny village, in 1834 produced 'Praise, my soul'. Yet another country Rector, John Keble, assembled a book of simple sacred poems in 1827, 'The Church's Year', which proved to be a best-seller, and although he thought of these as devotional poems adapted to the church seasons, many of them almost at once became well known hymns, like 'New every morning', and 'Sun of my soul.' Perhaps the finest of all was 'Ride on! Ride on in majesty', added to the collection of Heber's hymns posthumously published in 1827; but it was not by Heber: the author was Dean H.H. Milman.

> Ride on! Ride on in majesty;
> the winged squadrons of the sky
> look down with sad and wondering eyes
> to see the aproaching sacrifice. —

— you see there a new consciousness of the weight and sound of words, a new freedom of imagination, and this, when allied with a touch of that interest in natural sights and sounds which was so amply celebrated in Wordsworth, was the reason why so many hymns from that period remain among the best known and best loved of all. Indeed, these early anglican writers showed signs of becoming as good at their craft as some of the American writers (more about them in a moment) who were their near contemporaries. Doctrine — well, yes, doctrine does move back a little. 'Holy, Holy, Holy' isn't really a hymn about the doctrine of the Trinity of the kind Watts or Wesley would have written: it is a rendering into verse of the vision of the Book of Revelation. 'Bread of the world' isn't a Eucharistic hymn in the sense that 'Schmücke dich' of 'Nature with open volume' were — but what these writers did was to make hymnody friendly rather than hectoring and didactic and fierce, as the 18th century writers, when not at the top of their inspiration, were liable to be.

Non-anglican writers, especially Congregationalists, were still being energetic, and this period produced what is surely the greatest hymn of the Beatific Vision ever written by a non-anglican, Thomas Binney's 'Eternal Light!' — a hymn hardly known now in America, long treasured among non-anglicans in England, and just now becoming there known to anglicans. It took a combination of calvinist insight and romantic sense of distance to produce, from this Congregationalist minister, such stanzas as these —

O how shall I, whose native sphere
   is dark, whose mind is dim
before the Ineffable appear,
and on my naked spirit bear
   the uncreated beam?

There is a way for man to rise
   to that sublime abode —
an offering and a sacrifice,
a Holy Spirit's energies,
   an Advocate with God.

The Unitarians were also prominent; though much of their material tends to be a shade over-cultivated for congregational taste. Sir John Bowring, MP, surprises us all with 'In the Cross of Christ I glory' — a reaction, in hymns of the Atonement, against the evangelical tendency to be obsessed with the details of the Crucifixion, — and 'Watchman, tell us of the night', a dramatic hymn much loved in America.

VII

The Crisis of Liturgy

But suddenly a wind blew up from a quite new direction, and started scattering leaves and threatening even buildings. This was the Oxford Movement, and although it initially affected the Anglican church, no other main-line denomination in England was ultimately unaffected by it. To be brief, this new stirring of thought and devotion in the church of England, usually dated from the Assize Sermon of John Keble in 1833 entitled 'National Apostasy', consisted of a call, from a group of Anglican clergy, to the revival of a church whose lapse into triviality and irrelevance the Evangelicals had so ruthlessly shown up. Was there any answer to Evangelicalism, with its new styles of worship, its new enormous preaching houses, its fiery sermons, its tendency to all the errors into which pietism could fall once the firm hand of the Wesleys was removed?

Such an answer had to be direct and comprehensive. It included, in this case (a) A reconsideration of the accepted interpretation of 'Reformation' and of the total opposition of English churchmanship to what Rome stood for; (b) new standards of behaviour and devotion in the clergy, (c) a revival of liturgy, including principally a restoration of the Eucharist to its central place in worship, and (d) a total renewal of parish life and mission. As a result of this, said its first leaders, we shall achieve a new evangelization of the industrial masses, especially the poor of the new English industrial towns.

The typical product of the Oxford Movement is the often rather ugly but energetic Victorian church in what were at the time the English slums: where ceremonial, light, incense, the drama of the Eucharist, the authority of a celibate always-cassocked priest, the revival of confession, processions out of doors and indoors, the cult of the saints, and all the rest of what was recovered from the Middle Ages provided for the poor exactly the colour and vitality, associated with the security of dogma, that nothing else in their lives came near to providing. Let nobody think that this revival, led by J.H. Newman, John Keble, E.B. Pusey, Isaac Williams and a whole team of enthusiasts (not a few of whom ended as Roman Catholics) was merely an intellectual or aesthetic revival: at the bottom it was evangelical — but of course it suggested that the word 'evangelical' be radically reinterpreted. The traditional evangelicals replied vigorously, not only with the new foundations of Primitive Methodism, the Brethren, and similar movements, but with the Salvation Army and the imported revivals of Sankey and Moody. The counterpoint thus generated was not so much between Anglicans and the rest as between those, in many denominations, who wished to stick to the old pattern of evangelism and those who wished to revise it.

This changed the whole course of hymnody. The Anglicans now saw a need for two kinds of new hymn. They wanted first to develop the technique of Watts, Wesley and Montgomery for their own purposes —to produce a dogmatic statement, in popular language, of the faith as they now saw it. But they directed their first efforts towards a new image of hymn singing, which they sought to fashion by feeding into the church translations of all those Latin hymns from the Middle Ages which had been unknown to English singers ever since the Reformation. They began by translating them into English meters so that they could be sung to familiar tunes (the translators being Chandler, Caswall, Williams and others), then they went over the ground again, retranslating them so that they could go to the original plainsong. On the whole the older kind make better English hymns: such as 'O Christ our hope, our hearts' desire', 'Disposer supreme' and 'O Holy Spirit, Lord of grace' and the very pleasant 'Bethlehem, of noblest cities'. The restriction imposed by using the original meters caused some later versions to be pedantic and contrived, having their own branch of remoteness and stiffness as the metrical Psalms did, although J.M. Neale (1818-1866), the finest of these translators, often rose to real genius in his versions. But even he is often better when he abandons the old meters. In America the best known of his translations are 'O what their joy and their glory must be', 'O Love, how deep, how broad, how high', and 'Christ is made the sure foundation'. (The second of these is a joint composition by Neale and his friend Benjamin Webb). When he abandoned his rule of using the original metre he produced many 'winners', like 'All glory, laud and honour', 'Jerusalem the golden', and (from the Greek) 'Come, ye faithful, raise the strain', 'The day of resurrection' and 'Christian, dost thou see them.'

There really were people in this group who felt that the Church of England needed little of anything beyond the hymnody of the medieval church, supplemented by that of the 18th century Catholic revival (which gave us, among other things, 'On Jordan's bank'). But obviously this would not quite do: and after several people had privately attempted to produce a hymnal for the new-style Church of England, a small group of friends, headed by Sir Henry Baker, decided to launch, as a private adventure, a hymn book which would really bring together the archaistic and evangelistic aims of their movement. This was *Hymns Ancient and Modern,* which was to abecome the most famous hymnal in the world, and its first edition, of 273 hymns, (1861) was the opening of a dynasty which is still in active operation and which made its latest contribution to hymnody as recently as 1980.

This book was designed to be a hymnal illustrating the Book of Common Prayer, and it was exactly what its title claimed — a blending of the new and the old. It adopted a style of presentation — invented in England only in 1852 — by which the text of a hymn and its tune were printed together, not, as formerly, in separate books. It arranged the hymns exactly as the Prayer Book had been arranged, and number 1 has always been the morning hymn, 'Now that the daylight fills the sky.' It included all the medieval hymns required by the liturgy, and a fairly complete body of saints' day hymns; and on this foundation it built up a system of more modern hymnody including such pieces as 'As with gladness men of old' and 'Come, ye thankful people, come'. It looked for good poems that would make good hymns, and came up with Lyte's 'Abide with me' (1847) and Newman's 'Lead kindly light', setting them to tunes which at once carried them into people's lives. The editors decided which tune should go with which hymn, and had the absolutely new notion of setting 'Our God, our help in ages past' to the tune 'St. Anne' (a marriage performed when the text was 142 years old and the tune 153). They looked at hymns submitted, and at translations available, and unhesitatingly altered them where they thought they needed help in becoming popular: so they gave us the versions we know of 'O come, all ye faithful' and 'O come, O come, Immanuel'; the second of these is often further altered in American hymnals: but no user of it ever sings anything like what Neale originally wrote.

What was even more, they discovered a composer who had an unexampled felicity in finding his target in people's affections — J.B. Dykes, Vicar of St. Oswald's, Durham: seven of his tunes appeared in the first edition and among these are those we almost always sing to 'Eternal Father strong to save', 'Holy, Holy, Holy', and 'Lead kindly light'. They got the Mendelssohn tune safely married to 'Hark the herald angels sing'; a simple German chorale was comfortably settled with 'Forty days and forty nights', and 'O sacred head' (though not in the translation which most books now use, which is American) was safely launched into the English-speaking world.

Indeed they killed many more birds than two with one stone. They more or less settled the form in which English hymnals should appear (and American ones until about 1930); they introduced congregational singing to congregations which had almost forgotten how to do it; and they made popular a reserved, dignified style of hymn which nobody who knew only the evangelical hymns could imagine becoming popular. They turned their backs resolutely on what they called 'enthusiasm'; they meant by that, experience released from doctrinal control. But dogma was seven-tenths liturgy for them. So the hymns their successors produced, though sometimes masterly, tended to become so reserved as to be theologically inaudible. They were perhaps at their weakest when being didactic, and at their worst when writing for children.

> Within the churchyard side by side
> are many long, low graves;
> and some have stones set over them;
> on some the green grass waves.

That, for children, from the 1889 revision of this book, goes on to describe what the churchyard is for —

> They cannot hear when the great bell
> is tolling overhead;
> they cannot rise and come to church
> with us, for they are dead.

The author of that, Mrs. Alexander, also wrote 'There is a green hill' and 'Once in royal David's city' and 'All things bright and beautiful' — in all three of which there is at least one stanza which provokes all the wrong reactions now: everybody derides 'the rich man in his castle, the poor man at his gate'; we really can't now live with 'Christian children all must be mild, obedient, good as he.'

Things were not much better when the anxious authors had to try to find a hymn about the unknown Saint Bartholomew, or to translate medieval monkish pieces about saints who come through as so joyless and humourless as to be sub-human. And milder forms of didacticism often allowed romanticism to become unruly. What, after all, is 'For all the saints' (if one can possibly think of it apart from its magnificent tune, composed when the text was forty years old) but an impressionistic reminiscence of a Victorian heaven? It was once remarked by somebody interested in theology that the only theology in it is in the words 'by faith.'

An enormous anglican hymn-explosion, producing scores of hymnals, was the result of the Oxford Movement; but some of the best writing was done by people who were theologically well away from its center. One of the best hymns to come from an otherwise obscure 'central' source is F.S. Pierpoint's 'For the beauty of the earth'; but one might well say that much of 'The church's one foundation' is more substantial theologically, and this came from a young clergyman of 26 of what we would now call 'conservative' views who was greatly disturbed by the effect on the church (specifically on Bishop Colenso in South Africa) of Biblical criticism. It is indeed a profoundly biblical hymn, and now among the best known of all. Bishop Wordsworth, one of the several bishops who were hymn writers of this period, was not in the fullest sense a 'high churchman' but he wrote a number of valuable didactic hymns: the best, which ought to be known better, is perhaps 'See the conqueror mounts in triumph' (EH 145: AM 148). F.T. Palgrave, a critic and anthologist of great talent, wrote a few hymns, including the very delightful 'O Thou not made with hands' (EH 464, AM 259). A schoolmaster, Henry Twells, proved to be one of the most original hymn writers of the time: his evening hymn 'At even when the sun was set', though very long (eight stanzas originally) is, compared with most Victorian evening hymns, full of imagination and thought. Professors joined in the game — like Edwin Hatch, a Professor of Church history, who gave us 'Breathe on me, breath of God.' And some very good work indeed was done by women writers — who could not have had less to do with theological disputes; Harriet Auber's 'Our blest Redeemer', Charlotte Elliott's 'Just as I am', and above all Caroline Noel's 'At the name of Jesus' all have proved to have plenty of staying power, though two of them are usually musically depressing.

The most important writer of all, however, was Catherine Winkworth, who, as far as we know, never wrote a hymn of her own but proved the most successful translator of German hymns into English; but for her we would not have 'Now thank we all our God', 'If thou but suffer God to guide thee' or 'Praise to the Lord, the Almighty'. This, of course, had nothing to do with the Oxford Movement, and everything to do with the new interest in Germany generated in England by the presence of Queen Victoria's husband, the German Prince Albert. Other translators helped England to import a large number of German hymns — Frances Cox, Eleanor and Jane Borthwick, Emma Bevan and Richard Massie among them. Oddly enough the translation of Luther's 'Ein' feste Burg' always used in England was made by a very famous writer who wrote no other hymns at all — the essayist and critic Thomas Carlyle. (The American equivalent, equally good, is 'A mighty fortress', translated by F.H. Hedge a little later).

So not everything was under the guidance of what we might call the English Counter-Reformation; and the intense vitality of 19th century English hymnody, though it was very largely the work of anglicans, is partly due to the fact that not only one stream was flowing.

But undoubtedly it was here that the foundations of modern hymnody were laid. It was in this period that hymnals took their familiar shape, that far more tunes became known, that hymns became respectable as part of the anglican liturgy, that the idea of the hymn as something the lay Christian really *possessed* was born, and that the seeds of all the modern congregational sense of hymnody were sown.

For the real thing that underlay all the foregoing patterns that the explosion formed was the idea of the hymn as the congregation's folk song. To be a folk song it has to have a tune, and it has to have its own tune. To be a congregational folk song it has to be a community song. What had impeded this in earlier days was the fact that where hymns were sung congregationally (and we must remember that this doesn't apply to the great majority of the Wesley hymns in the 18th century), a repertory of a dozen tunes could make a whole hymnal viable. Outside Wesley, apart from the experiments of Heber, you still had about half a dozen metres for almost all your hymns: so the musically indolent English could sing all those without knowing more than a dozen tunes. Tune books existed, of course, containing a hundred or two hundred tunes — the gesture of Novello in issuing four books in series of a hundred each between 1835 and 1843, called *The Psalmist,* was designed to be a great advance. But the ordinary parish got along with a barrel-organ that played perhaps twenty-four tunes, and probably didn't use even all those. But once the idea got about that a hymn had *its* tune, even though it was in Common Meter,people could think of hymns as folk songs. (You don't often get several dozen folk songs or carols going to the same tune). So when, a little later, suggestions were made that 'the tune' for some hymn could be replaced by a better one, or anyhow a different one, people were already prepared to approach that suggestion as if somebody had thought of altering the tune to 'Charlie is my darling' or the National Anthem. Of course, *Hymns Ancient and Modern* was not anything like a hundred per cent efficient in its efforts: perhaps not more than twenty per cent. But if it was twenty per cent, that was a startling achievement.

This can be checked by observing one thing about hymn tunes that not everybody notices: that they all (except in some Roman Catholic circles) have names. Having noticed this, you find that in a large number of cases if the tune is German the name is a German phrase like 'Nun danket' or 'Herzliebster Jesu' which is the opening words of they hymn it goes with. The German system from the first was to set one tune to one hymn and let the marriage stay undisturbed. But the English tunes (and the American ones and Scottish ones) are names after places, or saints, or people, or occasionally with abstract words, like 'Dundee', or 'St. Anne', or 'Alford' or 'Rest'. This goes back to 1621, when the English editor Ravenscroft saw that there was no settled association for so many tunes that they had to have, as it were, a license-plate for identification. In 1621 he would call a tune 'Old Hundredth' because it was indeed the indivorcible tune for the Hundredth Psalm in the old official metrical version; but common metre tunes he had to give names like 'Dundee' simply to identify them. It was as simple as that.

One other quite different movement helped establish the folksong character of the English hymn; this was the invention of community singing, which received its greatest impetus in the 1840s under John Mainzer and John Hullah; at the time this was variously called 'The Singing Mania' and 'Hullah-baloo'. These two impresarios of amateurism, the Lowell Masons of Britain, working quite independently, started singing classes all over the country, much helped by the invention of the 'Tonic sol-fa' letter-note system of singing (which corresponds to what in the USA is now called 'solfege'). People in the new cities gathered in choral societies, and produced a demand for easy church music which appeared in the form of cantatas, anthems, glees and part-songs, many of which are now regarded only as monuments of pedestrian or empty-headed music. The noncomformist churches — especially the large ones in the cities — were often centres of this new music-making, and their congregational singing was nourished by them. Congregational singing in four parts was now entirely accepted, as in some places was the congregational singing of the anthems in services. The last nonconformist hymnal to be published with anthems bound in appeared in 1916 — The *Congregational Hymnary:* 771 hymns, a hundred or so psalms with anglican chants, and a hundred anthems on top of that: a good solid volume.

So everybody was singing hymns: not, in different denominations, by any means the same hymns. But everybody wanted hymns; and of course a sudden demand produced mass-produced goods, so there grew up a jungle of semi-popular hymnody, which almost stifled the growth of hymns of the standard we got in earlier days. Easy to write, easy to compose, easy to publish, and easy to get widely sung, hymns became a national industry. The surprising thing turns out to be that so many of them were good hymns.

Among anglican offerings we have not mentioned already, from the period 1860-1900, one would surely include as good examples 'The King of love', 'Bright the Vision', 'Alleluia, sing to Jesus', 'O worship the Lord in the beauty of holiness', 'The day thou gavest': and the tunes 'Regent Square' (Christ is made the sure foundation), 'Irby' (Once in royal David's city), 'St. Albinus' (Jesus lives!), 'Lancashire' (in the US, 'The day of Resurrection) and 'Praise, my soul' (in US called 'Lauda Anima'). Among resoundingly successful hymns of which the present generation is understandably shy, we could also mention 'Onward Christian soldiers' and 'Fight the good fight': and everyone of the text we have just mentioned was the work of an anglican' clergyman, and all the tunes were by anglican organists.

VIII

The Varied Scenery

The pattern is now quite obvious: hymns are at their most energetic and creative when the pressure is on. The primitive church: the Reformation: Pietism: Methodism: Puritanism: Olney: The Oxford Movement. The standard of fervor and intensity sags when the pressure is off and hymn singing becomes an establishment activity.

We can fill in that picture as we go back a little in time and pick up some information about one or two unusual kinds of hymnody. We can begin by mentioning two sources of hymns which are familiar to contemporary readers because they have sent their products through the frontier which their cultures were content to establish. I mean in the first place the Welsh hymnody and in the second, what is known as American folk hymnody.

Welsh hymnody is known outside Wales only through its music. We have already said that just one Welsh text is known outside Wales in translation: 'Guide me, O thou great Jehovah.' There have indeed been very few Welsh-speaking writers who wrote in English — the most distinguished must have been Howell Elfed Lewis (1860-1953), the distinguished Welsh bard who wrote in both languages and some of whose English hymns should be better known in the USA than they are.

Welsh history has been a matter of legend and mystery so far as the English are concerned, right down to the Industrial Revolution. Mountainous, until recently almost inaccessible, barren, tough, remote, Wales was for many centuries a culture of villages: originally, indeed, a culture of tiny monasteries. The Welsh people are the ancient British people evicted by the raids of the Saxon races between about 450 and 1000 A.D., and Welsh like to refer to England as a new settlement to the east of Wales. The Welsh culture is a culture of speech and song, not of writing.

Everybody who knows hymns takes delight in the great Welsh hymn tunes — 'Hyfrydol', 'Llangloffan', 'Aberystwyth', 'Ebenezer', 'Joanna' (sometimes called 'St. Denio'), 'Gwalchmai', 'Llanfair', 'Rhosymedre'. . . . The procession of fascinating and (to the uninitiated) unpronounceable names rolls past and the sounds, once heard, are unforgettable.

Now all the Welsh tunes we know best come from the time, or show the effects, of the Welsh Evangelical Revival. This Revival is very closely associated with the English one led by the Wesleys, but it would be a mistake to claim that without the Wesleys it would not have happened. Welsh evangelists were already in business by 1738, and were only waiting for the fresh input of energy provided by the Wesley preachers to make the revival a national effort. And the earliest Welsh hymn tunes have all the confidence and cheerfulness of the first English revival tunes: indeed, people have found the origins of some of them in the same popular operatic music that inspired the contents of the early Wesley tune books. Early Welsh tunes tend on the whole to be like 'Joanna' (Immortal, invisible) and 'Llanfair' (Praise the Lord, his glories show); it is towards the mid-19th century that we have an outpouring of those grave and ardent minor-key melodies which strike non-Welsh people as most characteristically Welsh — such tunes as 'Bryn Calfaria' ('Lord, enthroned in heavenly splendor'), 'Aberystwyth', ('Jesus lover of my soul'), and 'Llangloffan' ('O God of earth and altar'), — behind which there is an endless series of similarly evocative and beautifully-formed tunes.

The Welsh, we all say, are innately musical. They are indeed, in the sense that they make music naturally, as naturally as speaking. Their music is in that way true folk music; a group of Welsh people — traditionally, Welsh *men* — make harmony with instinctive precision. This, anyhow, was true in the 19th century when Welsh hymnody reached its highest point of inspiration. The evangelical movement, which had in England mostly to sing to large numbers of people often in the open air, found in Wales groups of people huddled in small village chapels waiting to sing themselves. It is still possible to hear Welsh worshippers at a Welsh-language service rejoicing in hymnody in a manner quite different from what we find in England or in the northern states of America. Quite often where one would expect a hymn, they sing three hymns. They express their religion in a kind of ecstatic hymnody which is peculiar to a certain kind of environment.

The Welsh are, we said, innately musical: but that is not the whole story. The environment from which 'classic' Welsh hymnody comes is a closed environment into which what the English (for example) would call social mobility never enters. When Welsh hymns are heard thus sung, and Welsh worship is thus held outside the Welsh villages, it becomes a retreat into a racial memory: a recovery for a while of an emotional and religious climate from which the Welsh are exiled. In many parts of Wales now what used to be typical Welsh singing is a survival in an alien culture of something which still has roots but no longer bears leaves or blossom.

The nearest parallel in accessible hymnody seems to me to be the 'folk hymnody', as it is called, of the Appalachian valleys of the USA. You do not there hear the same sounds you hear in Wales; but hymns are sung in the same way, by the same kind of people: very poor people, isolated partly by geography and partly by choice, people who neither have nor value what others call education. Massive hymn-singing sessions are part of the life of the Tennessee valleys still. Sociologists have shown how this culture is being invaded by the mobile culture of the rest of the USA, and to what an extent the shape-note hymnody of these communities is a survival in a now alien climate.

Oddly enough, the sound made at these hymn-singing sessions, so closely related to the Welsh 'Cymanfa ganu', is not what anyone can call beautiful; it is nasal, hectic and inexpressive, and about as far as it could be from the sound of a Welsh choir. This fact is what makes us cautious about attributing the special character of Welsh hymns only to 'innate' musical talent. What is really happening in both fields is the generation of lively hymnody by the force that comes of religion being pressed through a narrow channel: and that is what all through our story we have been observing. It is a narrow channel, or a carefully defined space, that causes the pressure to rise, and during the 19th century we begin to see the most spectacular vindications of this principle. The more heartily you sing, it begins to appear, the less religiously hospitable you are likely to be.

Certainly this is true of the old-style Welsh and of the 'poor whites' of the Tennessee valleys. So is another thing: the fact that the music of these communities took quite a while to travel outside them. You will find almost no Welsh hymn tunes in English hymn books before 1900, although they were being coined from soon after 1730; and you will find almost nothing from the 'shape note' tune books of the American South-East in 'standard' hymnals before about 1955. 'Amazing grace' was one of the first to become widely popular, and it was the Billy Graham crusades, from the early 1950s, that released that particular tune from the valleys. More recently the scholars have been moving in and discovering in these strange hymn books melody after melody which, re-scored the language of 'standard' music, captivates increasing numbers of congregations.

This is called 'folk hymnody' and Welsh hymnody could carry the same name. The expression means that it is hymnody that 'comes natural' to people in certain well-defined communities. It means that nobody, in the communities to which it properly belongs, cares who wrote which tune. If names of composers are attached, they are often speculative. They are often still listed as 'American folk hymn.' In just the same way, people were content to call Welsh tunes just 'Welsh Hymn tune', before researchers discovered, as some have recently done, to whom they could be attributed. The crowning example of the 'folk' nature of hymnody is, of course, the tune 'Ebenezer' (sung in America to 'Once to every man and nation'). This first appeared in an English hymn book in 1906: the book was the *English Hymnal* and it called it simply 'Welsh hymn melody.' Those scholarly researchers who took such trouble to verify the sources of English and German tunes had simply no idea that its composer was thirty-seven years old at the time. More than that, however: somebody put about the story that the tune was found on the coast of South Wales in a bottle washed up by the sea, and it became known as 'Ton-y-botel'. Nobody thought it necessary to ask what its composer thought about that; Thomas John Williams had in fact composed it about 1890 as part of an anthem — but people would rather believe anything but that a Welsh hymn tune was composed by an identifiable person.

Folk hymnody is community hymnody: it is the folk song of an identifiable religious group — and it's the identifiability that matters. Folk song takes on its own venerable mystique — appropriate to anything whose origins one doesn't know; it becomes quite easy not to want to know.

Let us take this a few steps further. Consider on the one hand the mystique of the Afro-American Spiritual, and on the other, that of what Americans call the 'Gospel Song'. Both have a very strong and observable character, and both belong to identifiable communities. The Afro-American Spiritual is the property of the African slaves evangelized by white missionaries. It combines an African intensity of rhythm and phrase form with a manner, at once brooding and ecstatic, which bespeaks the sufferings and hopes, the visions and heroisms, of the submerged Black community in the American slave-owning states. The 'Gospel Song', essentially a nursery-rhyme with a chorus, a kind of latter-day carol, belongs first to the camp-meeting evangelical crusades of the earlier 19th century, then to the more institutional evangelical bodies affected by the Second Evangelical Awakening of 1859. Observe the 'evangelical' factor that is common to both. That religious style which is usually called evangelical (though this is a secondary and etiolated meaning of the word) normally uses the technique of constructing an identifiable community out of those whom they evangelize. The pattern is to bind people closely together, partly by inducing a common ecstasy of religious emotion and partly by urging their converts to keep themselves separate from the 'world' through various forms of abstinence and of conspicuous behaviour and speech. If the community didn't form itself, or wasn't formed by a chain of historical accidents (as the communities of the Tennessee Valleys were, and as those of the Welsh villages were), it is always possible to manufacture a frontier which will mark off the new evangelizing body.

This, undoubtedly, is what provided the ground in which Fanny Crosby (Mrs. van Alstyne: 1820-1915) sowed her ten thousand hymns. But we will take yet another step, and ask what happens when the community either breaks up, or allows its nature to be altered. Well: it is plain fact that 'typical Welsh' tunes are not being composed now: they are as completely locked up in history as Genevan Psalms. If anyone in fact goes to the South East of the USA and attends these hymn-singing marathons, or listens to the famous recording of the *Sacred Harp* (that refers to the most massive of all the American *cymangfa ganau* or singing festivals), one may well be surprised at the absence from the program of what one expected to hear, as examples of the innocent beauty of Southern Folk Hymnody: one may receive the same sort of shock which I received in south Wales when, being invited to conduct a singing festival, I found that the program contaied only one Welsh tune and no Welsh texts at all.

Compare this, from the Introduction to the new edition (1978) of an old shape-note hymnal, *The New Harp of Columbia* (1867); the writer is Dorothy D. Horn.

> I once drove to a rural section of Indiana to hear a widely publicized yearly singing in which the descendants of the original pioneers met to re-create the singing school that had played an important part in the lives of their ancestors. What I heard was the most unmitigated musical tripe: songs celebrating the beautiful spring, true love, or whatever, and tearjerkers relating to the death of a loved one, all set to the tritest of tunes. On inquiry I found that the original singing school had used the wholly admirable *Missouri Harmony,* but in the 1880s the younger members had demanded something more elegant.

Even in the authentic 'Sacred Harp' tradition, one hears now (if the record is anything to judge by) more of the imitative 'fuguing' tunes based on a decadent English evangelical tradition than of the true folk hymnody of the original settlers.

'More elegant' — that was a revealing phrase. The Afro-American Spirituals of the 1797 Kentucky Revivals have not much place in the worship of modern urban Afro-American communities. The 'more elegant' cadences of Victorian English and 19th century American music are heard much more often. The 'Gospel Songs' originally devized to teach the almost illiterate southerners the basics of Christianity are now the property of four-figure-membership Baptist Churches, and the newer compositions in their style are the stock in trade of the aggressive evangelical crusades of to-day.

But there is even yet another thing to be said about these streams of folk-hymnody; and that is that three of them, the Welsh, the Appalachian and the Black, are associated in their origins with suffering. The communities that generated them were forced together by the pressure of poverty. The 19th century rustic Welsh were poor: the Highland-Clearance Scots who ended up in North Carolina and East Tennessee were abysmally poor: the Black people were worse than poor.

You could say that all those three kinds of folk hymnody were balm for the wounded and comfort for the dispossessed and songs of the homeland for the exiles. But then consider: the English (and the bourgeois American) swoons over the beauty of the Welsh hymn tunes; and we take great delight in the melodies of the authentic Appalachian hymns; and we are moved by the pathos of the Black Spirituals. Does this means that we are projecting on to them the 'elegance' we crave for? Well, quite certainly, in our semi-secular reactions to the admirable singing of Welsh choirs, (the best ones are still choirs of miners), to the shapeliness of tunes like the one now much loved for 'My shepherd will supply my need', and to the drama of 'Swing low, sweet chariot', we are re-categorizing those songs as entertainment for our sophisticated ears.

A certain caution is necessary in approaching all these. But that leaves the Gospel Songs to be dealt with; and history seems to insist that these from the first were not songs indigenous to a natural group but songs imposed on an artificial group — a community whose identity was prescribed by the zealous evangelists. I do not associate suffering with the origin of Gospel Songs, though we must all admit that they brought great comfort to the poor of Britain when Sankey and the Salvation Army made our industrial gloom a little lighter by using them.

We have found our journey taking an unexpected turn; and we cannot possibly say that what we are now looking at is the whole scenery of hymnody. Specifically, nothing like all creative hymnody was born of suffering, and nothing like all of it comes from underprivileged people. It can just as easily be born of bigotry as of misery. It can just as easily comfort the pharisee as the publican.

But what these rather dramatic scenes tell us, surely, is this: that hymns *as entertainment* are a very dubious self-indulgence; and that when specially straitened circumstances produce powerful folk-hymnody, that hymnody becomes in a special way vulnerable. Tension of any kind, whether in the form of suffering, or simply of the conflict of ideas, becomes most dangerous when it is uncontrolled at either end; it becomes like a broken belt in a high-powered machine or like an exploding boiler. It is possible, we all know, to be entertained and edified by the dramatic presentations of tensions and sufferings which we ourselves do not experience; but here is always the danger of addiction to the sensation without responsibility in one's use of it. That becomes sentimentality, a cruel vice because a smooth-faced one.

I myself suspect that it was a half-formed consciousness that something of that sort was going on that produced what we now call the study of hymnology. Certain it is that a critical approach to an activity which everybody, in different ways, had taken for granted as part of the scenery of worship, began to make itself felt towards the end of the 19th century. And although it is customary for people who now engage in this activity at any level to say that the phenomenon of early 20th century hymnody was a reaction against the habits and culture of the English Victorians, the story is much more complex than that; for it was during that century that we discovered just how degenerate hymnody could become, and, what was worse, how degenerate hymn-singers could become. The use of the word 'hymn-singing' as a pejorative adjective is appropriate to, and was given currency, in the social climate in which Dickens wrote his novels. It was not only Victorian country congregations who were sentimental; so were the industrual evangelicals. And so were the third and fourth generations of those who had coined the Spirituals, the Folk hymns, and Gospel Songs.

We have entered America, you might say, by a back door: not, anyhow, by the route the Pilgrim Fathers took. We may as well remain there for a while longer and notice what was happening in the more sophisticated and metropolitan parts of the United States. During the period before 1776 there was very little native hymnody in the Colonies; and during the first century of Independence the successive waves of immigrants brought their own cultures, and their own languages with them, and did not get far towards achieving that measure of integration which the USA now enjoys. There was, of course, the hearty and fervent and nostalgic hymn singing which we have just learnt to associate with defined communities. It is still there in the Mennonite congregations —who preserve their tradition of unaccompanied singing as a brave gesture against the entirely metropolitan and cosmopolitan influence of the organ. But in New England and New York State that first century was a time of intellectual supremacy and energy. New England had been forming itself since 1620 — it had 150 years' start on some of the other States and nearly 300 years' start on the State of Oklahoma. Perhaps it is surprising that in that settled and confident society so few of the arts flourished. Those that did were literature and rhetoric — the argumentative and pedagogic arts. If William Billings and Jeremiah Ingalls are in the front rank of indigenous musicians, one feels that it was a slow start.

But in the period 1776-1876 hymnody was nourished precisely by the argumentative and pedagogic energy of the New Englanders. There was no State Church, but there certainly was an unacknowledged Establishment, and it was a freethinking yet religiously fervent Establishment. Preachers of abundant mental equipment attracted congregations who wanted to think, or at least wanted to celebrate the freedom of thought and imagination. It is no accident that some of the best literature in American hymns at the time was written by Unitarians —'City of God', for example, and 'I look to thee in every need.' Other excellent hymns were written by Congregationalists who were often not far from being Unitarians: like Ray Palmer's admirable 'My faith looks up to thee' and his translation, 'Jesu, thou joy of loving hearts'. The Quakers, the most blissfully undogmatic of all Christian companies, produced in John Greenleaf Whittier a poet of social passion and literary grace from whose works many hymns were taken almost as soon as they appeared: 'Immortal love', 'Dear Lord and Father of mankind', 'O Lord and Master of us all', 'O brother man.' A young student of Andover-Newton Seminary wrote for his graduating class 'Eternal Ruler of the ceaseless round' — majestic in its diction and thought; a Unitarian wrote the first Christmas hymn with a social message, 'It came upon the midnight clear' — and indeed there is a social message in the verse usually dropped from 'O little town of Bethlehem', written by the Episcopal Rector of St. Matthew's, Philadelphia, and later and better known as Bishop Phillips Brooks. Towards the end of the period a certain artificial confidence associated with the first centennial in 1876 produced a rather more inflated style, as in 'Ancient of days' and 'God of our fathers, whose almighty hand' — but on the whole it was excellent literature, if dogmatically unreliable.

But the musicians let them down. Not that they did not match them in energy; but they lacked any sort of creative quality. We can say that now, because we can see how much there was to admire in what they did. Lowell Mason, Thomas Hastings, Henry S. Cutler, Virgil C. Taylor — they were all at their best when they were not composing.

Where the literary men and women brought the argumentative and expository faculties of puritanism to the level we associate with Emerson, Thoreau and Oliver Wendell Holmes, the musicians committed themselves to the pedagogic calling: and in this they had large and wholly admirable success. Lowell Mason was their patriarch, and he, his colleagues and his pupils, set up a network of singing schools a decade before the similar schools were brought to England by Mainzer and Hullah. Indeed, it was their example which gave great impetus to that singing movement in the south on which we were commenting earlier. Shape-notes were actually invented in New England, before mason's time. But — the old rule again — it was Mason who turned local enthusiasms into state-wide operations. As founder of the Boston Haydn and Handel Society he got those staid and self-sufficient puritans in Massachusetts interested in singing: and anything that could be sung, they sang with delight. Mason's ideas of church music were much loftier, and at the same time much more modest, than the ponderous pedestrianism of almost all his compositions would suggest. Hastings, who left with us a tune for 'Rock of Ages' which is only now attracting even slight protest, did almost as much as Mason to make people enjoy music. But the fact remained that the Founding Fathers were much too busy founding to give much thought to such details as hymnody; and there was not all that much energy left over for reflection once the duties of industrial expansion and religious activism were done.

The metropolitan hymnody of the early USA is oddly different from that of Britain: but the difference is easily explained. In the 1830s and 1840s the Establishment was puritan in New England; in Old England it was a new and energetic brand of anglicanism. There was, even in the 19th century, more respect for the past in England than in Boston. And then, we must face it, America never had a J.B. Dykes, to catch and reflect as exactly as he did the mood and temper of a majority-church. That is why American 19th century hymnody has that very curious touch of cold sentimentality about it, especially in its music. It is also why, in default of any sign of true native genius, imports like Beethoven's 'Ode to Joy' were drafted into service as hymn tunes. American metropolitan hymnody was much more like English nonconformist hymnody (Methodists apart) — and for the same reason. Both were the folk song of urban success, of a society whose positive virtues were in the area of enterprise, self-improvement and administration rather than of imagination or of religious contemplation.

IX

Too Good to Last

I am writing these words as 1980 slithers down towards the winter solstice, and I have just checked that it is 105 years since John Ellerton (the author of 'The day thou gavest') addressed a group of clergy and other interested people in 1875 'On Hymns and Hymn Singing.' For about a generation before this, people had begun to show interest in the history of hymns: the first 'Companion' to a hymn book, offering information about its contents and authors, seems to have been put together in 1845 in England and the second in 1846 in America. But now there is a rumour about that people are going to ask 'What is a *good* hymn?' Up to now people have perhaps asked, when editing hymnals, 'What available hymns will best suit my purpose?' But Ellerton started something when he addressed that meeting in the English West Midlands.

Ellerton was a gentle and learned Rector. A more strenuous mind was that of an English Congregationalist, Wiliam Garrett Horder, who in 1889 wrote a famous book, *The Hymn Lover,* surveying the whole history of hymnody and making the point that if English people wanted to refresh their hymn-vocabulary they could do worse than notice what the Americans were doing. To Horder belongs the credit for releasing into England many of those American hymns which are now favourites in both countries (and, as a sort of reciprocal offering, of making lines from an American poem by James Russell Lowell into the hymn we now know as 'Once to every man and nation' and exporting it back to the United States).

Then came, in 1892, the first edition of Julian's *Dictionary of Hymnology;* in its original form (with the supplement of 1907) one of the most forbidding one-volume books ever marketed: but a landmark, none the less. Hymnology was in business. It mattered who wrote what and when, and whether a story about a hymn was truth or gossip.

These prepared the way for further study, but not for the thunderclaps that came in 1899 and 1906 — two detonations but a single reverberation:

'The *English Hymanl* is a collection of the best hymns in the English language...
'[Good taste] is a moral rather than a musical issue.'
Those two quotations come from the Preface to the *English Hymnal (1906):* the first from the opening of the part written by Percy Dearmer, its chief editor, the second from the musical section written by the musical editor, Ralph Vaughan Williams.

The most formidable apostle of new standards was Robert Bridges, who later became Poet Laureate of England, and was the second of only two major English poets to interest himself in hymns (the other was Cowper). Bridges, precentor of the choir in a small village church at Yattendon, just outside Oxford, had in 1899 published for his congregation a hymnal supplement, the *Yattendon Hymnal,* and commenting on the principles he followed in compiling it he wrote, in the same year:

> The use of undignified music for sacred purposes may perhaps be justified in exceptional cases, which must be left to the judgment of those who consider all things lawful that they may save some. But if from the mission service this licence should creep into the special service, and then invade very act of public worship, it must be met with an edict of unscrupulous exclusion.*

Bridges complained loudly and constantly of the triviality of hymn music, and his prescription for its improvement recalled hymn singers to the historic heritage which in the spate of new and fashionable material that flooded the Victorian hymnals had been washed clean away. Dignity, integrity and authenticity were what he missed and what he sought to restore.

It was the *English Hymnal* that popularized these principles — not without having to encounter some weighty opposition in its first years. But Percy Dearmer, its editor, was an anglican priest zealous for the restoration of authenticity to the anglican liturgies (and for the correcting of errors which had been made by the first generation of Oxford reformers), and when it occurred to him to make a new hymnal to challenge the near-monopoly of *Hymns Ancient and Modern,* he set out on one of the most important cab-drives outside the Sherlock Holmes stories, to the address where the young and unknown musician Vaughan Williams lodged. Fifty years later Vaughan Williams recalled that Dearmer invited him to be the music editor of a new hymnal and

---

A Practical Discourse on Some Principles of Hymn Singing (Journal of Theological Studies Vol. I #1). Bridges's spelling, which was idiosyncratic since he advocated a system of spelling-reform which nobody took seriously, is here altered to the familiar style.

that he replied, 'I know nothing about hymns.' 'That', answered Dearmer — once again recalling that fictional sage — 'is why I am asking you to do it.'

One thing was obvious to a musician who was outside the fashionable circle of hymn-editors. This was that even if *Hymns Ancient and Modern* had a reasonably educated 'spread' of styles in its words and music, the total effect was one of decorous monotony. They all looked and sounded much the same. This was because the editors of 1861-1889 had not shaken off the evangelical tendency to adapt and re-fashion old material into a style agreeable to their constituents. The whole thing, they might have said if they were living now, was like an airline meal: whatever taste or tang there was in the original was usually removed in the cooking. To some extent this was true of the texts: much more was it true of the music. So those two entered on the task of enlarging the congregations' vocabulary and refining their taste. It was not a matter of composing and writing new things; Dearmer contributed some translations, and one first-rate hymn, 'Jesus, good above all other,' Vaughan Williams did a good deal of harmonizing, but wrote only four new tunes for the book. Four out of a total of 630 tunes remains an all-time low for a hymnal editor: but when one realizes that these tunes were set to 'For all the saints', 'Come down O love divine', 'Hail thee festival day', and 'God be with you', and are now closely associated with those texts almost all over the singing world, one realizes with what acuteness and judgment the new editor approached his work. Indeed, one has only to turn to 'For all the saints' in those hymnals which print both Vaughan Williams's tune and the one it was designed to replace (by Joseph Barnby) to see the difference Vaughan Williams hoped to make. It is now surely inconceivable to most people that the older tune should have been preferred to the new one as a setting of that cheerful, if theologically lightweight, text.

The two men saw things the same way. Dearmer, too, felt that the mediocrity of the contents of hymnals available to anglicans was bringing hymnody — the most memorable part of religious observance — into disrepute. It was, to his mind, cautious and conventional and dull. But his plan for improving it consisted not so much in finding new things as in restoring the salty savour of the work of past ages. On the whole he preferred unadulterated texts to altered ones, even where the original was quaint, just as Vaughan Williams preferred authentic to adjusted versions of the old psalm tunes, the Bach settings of chorales to Victorian settings, and above all the innocence of secular folk song to the tired and in-grown style of the second rate 'popular hymn tune.'

Perhaps the most interesting way in which Dearmer sought to fertilize anglican hymnody was in his use of so many American hymns discovered by Garrett Horder: he was enabling anglicans to sing for the first time 'Immortal love', 'Once to every man and nation', 'City of God', 'O little town of Bethlehem', 'Dear Lord and Father', and many more. He did, however, look round for new authors, and in printing for the first time Scott Holland's 'Judge eternal' and G.K. Chesterton's 'O God of earth and altar', he not only broke new ground but found two hymns, both written by people who never wrote other hymns, that have travelled all over the English speaking world.

The crusade that accompanied the appearance of this book was fiercely conducted by Dearmer and by his organist, Martin Shaw; and indeed it was associated with a movement that sought to purge all public art of vulgarity and tawdriness. The League of Arts, as it was called, proceeded on the belief that there was no reason why what was popular should be degenerate. The aim may have been too high and its expressions too diversified to make much difference in England's secular life: but in hymnody it had resounding success. This was because on the whole church people in England were ready to listen; the period 1900-1950 was the great period in England of intelligent lay Christianity, and it was the twenties and thirties that prepared people for what now looks like the astounding phenomenon of C.S. Lewis. There was just that combination, in the pews, or in enough pews to make an impression, of intelligent criticism and a readiness to give respect to any authority which was deemed to have earned it, that made it possible for hymnody to undergo radical change for the better.

There was, we might add, a new respect for dogmatic theology among the laity: an attitude to the Christian faith, for which we can largely thank the theological writings of Karl Barth, that expected dogmatic theology to be humane and severe: that saw in a quite new way how red-blooded and fascinating dogma could be. And, of course, there was plenty of social conscience and impatience of cant.

All this was assisted by the remarkable effect on public taste, in this field anyhow, of education. Education took two main forms: that which the young received at school and that which everybody receives through broadcasting. By the 1920s Dearmer and his friends had the ear of authorities in both areas. Dearmer, Vaughan Williams and Martin Shaw brought out a generalized and amplified version of the English Hymnal, leaving out all the strictly liturgical material, and aimed to produce a book of which no English teacher in a school need be ashamed, and no music teacher either. They found for it the inspired title, *Songs of Praise,* and this became for a generation the main influence in the state schools, and the hymnal used for the regular services broadcast by the BBC. So when hymnals came to be revised, especially those of the denominations least affected by this cultural revolution, their editors were pressed by the young to include what they had learnt at school, and by the laity to include what they heard broadcast. Your present writer has personal recollection of such a committee being in session from 1944 to 1947, and of the frequency with which members advocated such hymns as 'Praise to the Lord, the Almighty', 'because the children all known it from school.' That hymn had up to then been excluded from the hymnals of that denomination.

Another way in which the repertory was widened by the same group of reformers was by drafting into the hymnals poetry which was not designed as hymnody. There had been, we recall, a long period, between the first metrical psalters and Isaac Watts, that is, 1562-1707, when English congregations had virtually no hymnody. But that period produced a great deal of Christian lyric poetry, which was often cast in simple strophic form and could be sung to manageable tunes. So we begin to see, after 1906, the names of George Herbert ('Let all the world', 'King of glory', 'Teach me my God and King', 'Come, my Way'), John Donne ('Wilt thou forgive that sin...'), Robert Herrick ('In this world the isle of dreams'), Henry Vaughan ('My soul, there is a country'), Edmund Spenser, ('Most glorious Lord of life') and Samuel Crossman ('My song is love unknown') appearing in hymnals; and, in *Songs of Praise,* many others. This experiment had been tried before on a very limited scale — you find Milton and Tennyson in the older nonconformist hymnals; but Dearmer and his friends explored the poets to very good effect; among later poets used as hymn writers we find Christopher Smart, William Blake, John Clare, F.W.H. Myers and Rudyard Kipling. It did not always work: some poems set to music in *Songs of Praise* never made successful hymns. But the best of the sacred lyrics thus used had the effect — exactly what Dearmer hoped for — of releasing hymnody from an increasingly in-group vocabulary, of linking it more closely with the best of religious culture, and of delivering it from the almost settled mediocrity which Hymns Ancient and Modern more or less stood for in 1900. Hymns A & M, indeed, had only in a few cases used non-hymnic verse as poetry — 'Abide with me', and the two poems of John Henry Newman, 'Lead kindly light' and 'Praise to the Holiest'.

The purpose then was to make familiar things beautiful and beautiful things familiar, and an examination of the English hymn books of the main-line protestant denominations from the Scottish *Church Hymnary* of 1927 to the *Baptist Hymn Book* of 1962 indicates quite clearly how secure the foothold of this new culture became.

Corresponding with the new interest in what past history had to offer was a merked recession in the writing of new English hymns during that period. The standard had been set so high by Bridges that hymn writers became a great deal more cautious. What there is, is usually very good: but there is not a great deal of it. You do not find in the new editions of the hymnals many hymns newly written for them. You do not even find that in the *English Hymnal*. The most strenuous hymn writers in the 1920s, 30s and 40s were Dearmer himself and Canon G.W. Briggs ('Christ is the world's true light'); Dearmer was wayward — always a good stylist but in is later years more theologically anti-dogmatic, and tending to rewrite well-known hymns to purge them of those evangelical thoughts with which he was never in sympathy. Briggs, on the other hand, was firmly evangelical, a great lover of Watts and Wesley, and many of his hymns are sturdy, sound and (the best ones) eminently lyrical. To my own mind, the finest hymn written in this period is by an author revered as a pastor but otherwise almost unknown as a hymn writer, Henry C. Carter, a hymn on Ephesians 6.10 ff written by a convinced pacifist, of which these are two stanzas:

> Give me, O Christ, the strength that is in thee,
> > that I may stand in every evil hour;
> faints my poor heart except to thee I flee,
> > resting my weakness in thy perfect power.

> Give me to see the foes that I must fight,
> > powers of the darkness throned where thou shouldst reign;
> read the directings of thy wrath aright,
> > lest, striking flesh and blood, I strike in vain.

Another writer celebrated in another field (Old and New Testament scholarship) but too little appreciated as a hymn writer is George B. Caird, whose two fine hymns, 'Almighty Father who for us thy Son didst give' and 'Not, Lord, thine ancient works alone' appeared in the fifties and have a biblical urgency worthy of Charles Wesley himself.

Tune-writing, however, prospered. There were plenty of fine texts resurrected from the past, but not all of them had worthy tunes. In *Songs of Praise* we have a great deal of new work by Martin Shaw and some fascinating new tunes by Vaughan Williams, of which only 'Kings Weston' ('At the name of Jesus') has become well known, and that mostly in America. Other composers eminent in secular music were, like the older poets, drafted in: not all of them wrote tunes congregations could sing, but John Ireland's 'Love Unknown' ('My song is love unknown') has certainly come to stay. More tunes, actually, were composed than could possibly be used; new editors tried new things which sometimes worked, sometimes did not. The most successsful of all was Cyril Taylor's 'Abbots Leigh' (in England associated with 'Glorious things', but in America becoming known to other texts) — first generally heard through broadcasting but printed on a leaflet in 1941 and in a hymnal in *Hymns Ancient and Modern,* 1950. Other fairly prolific composers whose work travelled outside its original sources were Walter K. Stanton, George Thalben-Ball and Eric Thiman.

The same period in America tells something like the same story but at a much slower pace. The chief difference, of course, is that the American churches have always been 'on their own', without direct influence on the schools and without benefit (with certain notorious exceptions) of broadcasting. So there was nothing in the general ambience of life to make church people aware that there were fields outside their experience to be explored. On the whole 20th century American main-line hymnals are less critical and more complacent than their English counterparts. I suppose that the books one would single out as being important advances on their predecessors — seeking to increase the pace of progress rather than to float on its natural stream — are the *Episcopal Hymnal*-1940 and the Congregationalist *Pilgrim Hymnal* of 1958. All the other main-line denominational hymnals look like the work of editors whose whole energy was absorbed in satisfying intractable committees and providing what fairly sluggish congregations would accept. You do not find, except in the books mentioned, much tendency to ask whether the traditional collocation of a tune with a text is the best possible, or whether the accepted (often disfigured) version of a text or tune needs examining.

The one chance which American editors ought to take, and which only two during the period did take, is that of providing good hymnody for the kind of congregation which the 20th century has more of less invented: the interdenominational and culturally rootless congregation of the campuses. Yale and Harvard set a good example: *Hymns for Colleges and Schools* (1956) from Yale, produces an anthology whose standards are of the most rigorous kinds; and the smaller *Harvard Hymn Book* (1964) has the same kind of outlook. But campuses in general rarely use these; indeed, the *Pilgrim Hymnal* is the favourite at present for campuses which are not obliged to be loyal to denominational ties.

But the situation in America is now so different, and so complex, that it must be commented on further as we go on. What we saw in both countries, however, is a movement, strenuous in one, somewhat fitful in the other, towards the establishment for hymnody of a new status: Christian lyric for intelligent and sensitive people who are prepared to listen and learn. There was, as it turned out, no chance of this lasting longer than it did: it was lucky to have two generations to work on.

Hymnody in other hymn-singing areas did not have a renaissance until the period through which we are at present living — except very briefly in Germany. The European Lutheran and Reformed traditions were both affected by the fact that all their finest hymnody came very early: Luther and the early pietists left a magnificent treasury of hymnody to which writers and composers after 1750 in Germany found it difficult to add anything. The Reformed Churches were wedded still to the Genevan Psalter. The Scandinavian churches depended almost entirely on translations from the German. Music in the 19th century took a line which brought it to its highest development in secular large-scale compositions, but which was totally alien to the folk song style that good hymnody needs. So on the continent we see a huge hiatus, which until the 1960s looked as it it might be without a far boundary at all. The exception was, however, the small body of hymnody produced by the German Confessional Church after 1933, when the Protestant churches which declined to enter into a concordat with Hitler came together in resistance. The small and precious hymn supplement, 'Wehr und Waffen', of 1934, contains a number of new texts and tunes which reflect the militant spirit of a persecuted church, and which, musically, show the direct influence of the classic chorales and of true folk music. This hymnody might have lasted had not history taken so abrupt a turn after 1945; but it does reflect the same spirit as that of the English renaissance in turning back past the degeneracy of the previous two centuries towards the true sources of German hymnody; and, as I can myself testify (having been for three years the organist of a German refugee congregation in Oxford during World War II), the rigors of the time generated in the congregations a new respect for the classic hymnody of their remote ancestors.

But this kind of thing can go on only for just so long.

X

The Crisis of Denial

And so we come to the age in which we now live. It is an age which foreshortens our view of history and makes all previous ages look equally remote and ancient. World War II made us all the illegitimate children of history; the straight lines which seem to form the pattern of our genealogy developed quirks and kinks — the connection is there, because it is physical, but it is a distorted and crooked connection now. It is not World War I which produced the quirks because World War I left an *affective* trauma: a sense of shock and of profound suffering, and the chief moral drive it left with Europeans was an urge to see that war of that kind should be abolished from the earth. World War II left a *moral* trauma: the driving force in the generation it left was a need to be disconnected from the values that had produced it: and that meant, of course, not only responding morally to a human situation that had generated Auschwitz, but dismantling whatever beauty and integrity had got mixed up with that situation.

Specifically, what had to be unplugged at once was the network of pedagogy and intellectual authority of a hierarchical kind. Specifically: what the seniors said (all of whom were responsible for the unique horrors of World War II) was to be distrusted. The old idea of the psalmist, 'Things that we have heard and known, that our fathers have told us, we will not hide them from their children but tell to the coming generation' (Psalm 78. 3-4) — that was denied more resolutely than it ever was denied in history. The nearest thing to it had been the aftermath of the Thirty Years' War.

The results of this over twenty-five years have been astounding. There has been on the one hand a liberation of creative talent; talent, that is, which perhaps was oppressed by the sheer weight and authority of a great tradition revived in the Renaissance period of 1900-50. There was also, of course, a great deal of disconcerting destructiveness. We must try as best we can to sort this out, and we may as well take the bad news first because it arrived first.

Historical dialectic insisted that the pedagogues should not have the last word. Christian eschatology insists that no mortal who says

79

'only the best is good enough' ever gets the last word. So the case against the lofty standards of 1900-50 had to be stated. There was one proposition in it which with hindsight we can see coming, and we have mentioned it. This is that the age of raised standards was also the age in which creative effort went into recession. Faced with the recovered delights of old material, which came to the congregations as new material, and with the gestures against mediocrity made by Bridges and Vaughan Williams, writers and composers poroceeded with greater caution. The hill was much steeper to climb than they had reckoned. Upon this point the new generation seized with avidity; and the new generation became as busily creative as its great-grandparents had been.

But they probably saw something else as well. This was that the ecumenical movement had systematically demolished many of those walls which enclosed the definable spaces that had been the arena of traditional hymnody. Church people were thinking spaciously rather than provincially. Baptist girls went to universities and fell in love with anglican boys. 'The ecumenical movement', its apostles said, 'is the great new fact of our time.' Education and the BBC were interdenominational. The douce and polished contents of *Songs of Praise* contrasted sharply with the rugged, idiosyncratic, and sometimes exceedingly provincial taste of, say, the *Methodist Hymn Book* of 1904. It occurred to the new generation that in this broad and often rather featureless ecumenical landscape it might be as well to put up a few buildings that might offer something like coziness.

So in the fifties we have the hymnody of protest. Looking back on what at the time seemed to be adventurous pioneering, I now feel strongly that a good deal of this was fugitive: it was an attempt, in the bleak and alarming days following the second World War, to give life some shape, but to do that by providing shelter.

Consider what happened in those days to 'folk song.' Go back sixty years and watch Lucy Broadwood, Cecil Sharp, Vaughan Williams and all the rest of them collecting folk songs from country people and noting them down for the Journal of the English Folk Dance and Song Society; or consider, long before, William Sandys trekking down to Cornwall in 1827 and rescuing for us 'The first Nowell' and 'A virgin unspotted'. Exquisite and refreshing all this was: but contrast it with the folk song of the new 'underground', the 'alternative society', the new young whose favourite places of meeting were cellars in London and Newcastle. Cellars! A rich and decisive gesture in flavour, surely, of privacy in a newly crowded world: as a new generation of farmers might reverse to-day's customs of tearing up hedges and knocking down walls in the name of economics. These people, huddled, zealous, protesting, made new songs: they either did not write them down, or scribbled them on odd bits of paper. They made fashionable the primitive and portable guitar. They cared nothing for copyrights and authentic texts: they sang songs and threw them away. The songs were about the things that were closest to them — war, injustice, social wrongs, a new comradeship. A new identity was formed for these people by the only possible process: building a fortified enclosure of protest against everybody who was not of their kind, a protest reinforced in other primitive ways, such as dress.

That great modern Christian troubadour, Sydney Carter, knew these people, and saw in their songs something which Christians could use: and the result was a stream of informal songs, almost all of protest, which have become very well known, and which were the focus of Christian attention in the mid-sixties. 'Lord of the Dance' is a protest against traditional Christian immobility; 'When I needed a neighbor, were you there?' implies — it never *says* — 'You sure weren't there.' Carter sang these songs in a voice deliberately protesting against the *bel canto* of the parish or cathedral choir; he noted them down and left others to harmonize them (not really Vaughan Williams's style?); and in his book, *Green Print for Song* (Stainer & Bell/Galaxy, 1973), which is the most important document of this culture, he explains and candidly exposes all the doubts and visions and uncertainties and protests that moved him to lead this fashion of creative writing. Himself the most genial and peaceable of men, he stood for a radical protest against what he found to be the spiritual inefficiency and, yes, the hypocrisy of conventional Christians.

Of a very different kind were the new evangelicals with their new-style Gospel songs. The first wave of this cult broke in the mid-fifties with the work of the Twentieth Century Church Light Music Group: this was originally a circle of composers, almost all clergy or ordinands, who sought to reclaim the young by offering them a new informal style of music to sing to their familiar hymns; a little later they provided the hymns as well. The first famous exponent of this was Fr. Geoffrey Beaumont (1903-70), who had all England talking for a short while about his Folk Mass (1957) and his hymn tunes deliberately written in the style of the popular music of his time. Another of the group, Patrick Appleford, wrote hymns and tunes a few of which, like 'Lord Jesus Christ', have proved to be more enduring. Now this was something different: it was essentially an offering made by learned, cultivated and devoted people towards the culturally underprivileged, and therefore much more in the direct line of the American Gospel Songs; it was precisely not music coming out of the underprivileged areas, but music brought into it.

The new music was more conspicuous than the new words; and perhaps it turned out to be something of a miscalculation, since the underprivileged at whom it was aimed turned out to be the newly affluent young to whom the style of Ivor Novello (roughly the style these good people used) was as alien as that of Bach. It was entertaining enough, but one does now question whether it delivered anything of comparable value to what it intentionally set out to destroy.

The next phase of this is to be found in such publications as *Youth Praise,* a hymnal offered, again, by evangelicals to the young in 1966. Here we have again a musical style which is broadly speaking updated Sankey and Moody, with two spiritual moods: the militant and marching, or the introverted and yearning. There is, about much of the music in such books, a militaristic thump which at once shows what was really happening. Here were some more barns being built in the new ideological prairies; here were gangs forming and crusades being urged: subculture was raising its protest against the too rarefied culture of ecumenism. To say that many of the movements which made use of this kind of deliberately naive music were interdenominational is no refutation of our present proposition; it was, as with pietism, a case of people finding identity in manageable groups urged on by leaders of charismatic gifts.

A great deal of this material was very ugly indeed. Some of it was imaginative, but not much. To look through collections of songs promoted in this area is to be confronted by page after page of music all in a single style; and that, of course, is what we feel when we leaf through a late 18th century evangelical tune book like John Rippon's *Collection* or the Hymn Book of the Lock Hospital.

Two further comments have to be made. One is to contrast the musical amateurishness of so much that was offered to the English young with what corresponded to it in Germany. For in post-war Germany there arose, about this time, a movement in theology and evangelism which was exactly as revolutionary as pietism had been —but in the opposite direction. This is the hymnody which one encounters in such collections as *Schalom* (Berlin, Burckhardthaus, 1971) and *Christen Lieder Heute* (Siebenstern-Taschenbuch, Hamburg, 1971). Young and progressive clergy in Germany repudiated the hymnody of pietism, and even looked critically on Luther himself, and promoted the composition of new lyrics and new music, usually scored for guitar, expressing the spirit of the new age. Though it is almost always simple and popular in style there is about this music, and about many of the lyrics, an underlying seriousness, a professional self-control, and therefore often a scintillating originality, for which one searches in vain in the English youth books of the period. There is plenty of crusading spirit in these groups; it is often associated with social and political views which would be looked on with much disfavour in the United States. The high pressure of purposefulness has there produced some worthy, if often rather ferocious, hymnody. And that, of course, reflects the difference between the attitude of Germans and that of English to the situation left by the end of the Second World War — into which we need go no further here.

The shape of things in the United States is importantly different from this, and we are not quite ready yet to comment on it. Returning to England, we have to make our second comment. This is that the whole development of what might have been a new folk hymnody in the church was bedevilled by the incursion into the field of a new kind of commercial entrepreneur, who saw profit to be made in what abruptly came to be known as the 'pop scene.' As soon as this happened, the word 'folk' became corrupted and distorted. Folk song is always song for a reasonably definable group of folk, and its most blessed characteristic is un-selfconsciousness and a complete innocence of self-importance. This was certainly true of the 'underground' folk song we spoke of. It may not have been elegant, but heaven knows it was not pretentious. It was a major calamity when the media and the promoters got hold of this amateur style and inflated it into a crowd-gathering cult. From the days of the Beatles — kidnapped innocents if ever such were born — to the present we have been tyrannized over and brainwashed by the infernally pretentious antics of over-adulated groups of singers and players who have managed fairly effectively to destroy the genuine originality and insight which were to be found in many of the original songs of the Beatles. The salt of protest was overlaid by the sugar of glamor, and there followed at once a terrible idolatry of the pop-star which corrupted folk art irretrievably; what by its nature was the chamber art of a small group became the hysterical adulation of thousands at a time, inducing hysteria in large crowds and legitimizing, through this new Establishment, every kind of licence and mindless destruction of the landmarks of civilized society. If it was a prairie before it was now a dust-bowl. When all had been written and said by well-intentioned intellectuals in defence of all this, what the 'bottom line' showed was a hideous snatching of immediate pleasure leaving a wasteland of grey misery for others to try and clear up.

The pop-stars became the new prophets and priests; some developed genuine musical skill: most paraded mediocre or almost non-existent talent: many made fortunes; many died sadly and squalidly and untimely. What might have been the new folk song of a new age became the most colossally baneful spectator-entertainment the world had ever seen, and not a single puritan voice was raised against it. Ruefully, one can see what the vintage puritans of the 17th century meant when they discouraged crowd-entertainments.

No puritan voice: and precious few religious voices either. If this appalling business had happened in other fields — let us say that in which the ecologists and environmentalists work — there would have been representations made to governments . Aerosol sprays of a certain kind were thought to be damaging the protective screen which shields us from the effect of the sun's energy on the human organism: don't make holes in that or you'll all be in danger of skin cancer. But consider what this pop-cult was making holes in! A generation was being brought up to believe that life was nasty, brutish and short, and that they might legitimately both complain to the gods that what they had a right to (long life) was being withheld from them, and seek immediate pleasure without thought of the consequences. There is no tolerable life for crowded places without self-denial; self-denial was abolished. There is no enduring enjoyment of beauty without a certain amount of self-forgetfulness. Then let beauty go. There is no wit or good conversation without understatement and courtesy. Never mind that.

So the effects of this were felt far beyond the immediate circles of the idols and their disciples. Christian worship became a hedonistic indulgence, presided over by leaders who, affecting a humble contempt for rank and authority, deceived themselves and many others into thinking that they were offering the laity a liberation long looked for: what actually happend was a substitution of the nice guy for the priest and of something approaching the pop-scene anarchy for liturgy. The instant sensation which the secular idols traded in was approved in churches: the mournful licentiousness which the idols paraded was translated into a contorted theological permissiveness. And the mischief of it all was, once the vile polluted waters of this flood touched the church, that the church was able to reach back into its store of experience and bring back Zinzendorf in all his pretentious splendors. So a form of church music and hymnody grew out of the older evangelical and pietistic hymnody which, beginning by offering vast crowds of people hymnody of an almost sinfully undemanding kind, went on to silence the people altogether and to punctuate crowded evangelical crusading 'worship experiences' with spectator-music, sung not by the people but to them by carefully-groomed religious pop-idols.

Over this ground the tyrants were able to strut: and strut they did. Vast followings reduced to mindless adulation were coaxed along by the hypnotic repetitive eloquence of leaders who built themselves up as media personalities, who shouted, crooned, smiled, and even wept at their audiences and cajoled them into a sordid spiritual hedonism of which perhaps the ugliest aspect was the great pleasure they invited them to take in the fate of the damned. The mighty robed choir, the throbbing electronic organ, the persuasive demagogue, the chesty crooning soloist, the spacious auditorium, the cut-rate moral superiority, the petrified intelligence, the paralysed spiritual muscles: the reduction of all morality to two or three errors associated with sex — why, what is all this but civil war between one media-boosted pop scene and another?

We have, clearly, been dealing here with a fashion which is most popular in the United States, though it is by no means unknown in Britain. The USA has nothing that exactly corresponds either to Sydney Carter's 'folk' or to the Beaumont/Appleford 'light music' (indeed, 'light music' is not an expression used in America). But it does have two streams of development in the general direction of popular music. One is that neo-evangelical stream we have just alluded to: and although we were referring to an extreme corruption of it, milder forms of 'Youth Praise' music are to be found here and there — especially, for example, in the series of song books put out by the F.E.L. (Fellowship for English in the Liturgy) company and mostly aimed at Roman Catholic congregations. A little more about the Catholic developments in a moment.

But in the USA there is such a powerful traditional stream of evangelical popular music, dating from the camp meetings and the Second Evangelical Awakening, that popular religion has really found no difficulty in extending that tradition, and the commercial market for new 'Gospel Songs' remains buoyant. Alongside this there is also much traffic in informal songs, and, as might well be expected, plenty of experiment with jazz idioms. Some of the more serious compositions in this form reflect a touch of that professionalism we associated with contemporary German hymnody: the most successful and ingenious composer and lyric writer in this style is probably John Ylvisaker, and the most impressive and best known of the songs to come out of the protest-years of the sixties is no doubt Peter Scholtes' 'They'll know we are Christians by our love.' A number of small supplemental hymn books apeared from about 1965 onwards providing new forms of music — in which the special fashion of this style, hymn and tune from the same hand, was often followed — and many of these collections contain protest songs of considerable influence and intellectual weight. A characteristically interesting collection had the title *Hymns for Now: A Portfolio for Good, Bad or Rotten Times,* which was originally an issue (Vol. 39 #1) of the *Worker's Quarterly* (July 1967). In it the lyrics are mixed up with catchy and socially eloquent illustrations.

This collection, and others like it, provides easy songs, with usually one-line score and guitar symbols, which groups pick up at once, and whose texts express the restlessness and the impatience with conventional customs that go with youthful vision. Social protest and the unity of the group are the main subject: 'We shall overcome' and 'Brothers, sisters, we are one' appear very regularly. This is the modern mode of those hymns which in older days spoke of Christians as an army, like

'Onward Christian soldiers'. The army image has little appeal for contemporary youth, but they cannot do without the group, or the gang, and so the most responsible of the songs produced by this generation are some of the best examples of 'barns in the prairies.'

XI

The Crisis of Custom

We must now consider the very special case of Roman Catholic hymnody. Obviously the most sensational change in the church scene during the 20th century was the Second Vatican Council (1962-4), which made, only partly by intention, such sweeping changes in the culture and outlook of the Roman Catholic Church. But we have not said anything about the hymnody of that church since we left it at the end of the Middle Ages.

The nature of the Roman Catholic Church is, of course, ecumenical: the old sense of that word is simply 'universal and inter-racial'; the sense in which it is often used now signifying the dispersal of hostility between denominations is a secondary sense. Since the nature of the Roman Catholic Church is ecumenical, in its classic form it has directed the thinking of people towards their membership of the One Church rather than towards their membership of the local church. Medieval hymnody, we saw, is associated with the monastery — the most important definable community within the total spread of the Catholic Church. Medieval monastic hymns were in the fullest sense songs of the closed and identifiable group. But they were sung by those attached to that group, not by those who lived outside it but visited the Abbey church for their devotions. The hymns formed a small repertory closely linked to the liturgy. There were not hymnals in those days but service books with the hymns written into the Offices. You did not *choose* hymns any more than you chose prayers; they were integral to the formula of worship.

After the Reformation and the Counter-Reformation there was a long period during which the forces of fragmentation were at work even within the Catholic Church. It was impossible for Catholics not to see what the effect of hymnody on the Lutherans and Calvinists had been. And although the official hymnody of the church maintained its liturgical ethos (though a good deal of it was discreetly revised and rewritten in the Missal of 1632), we do begin to find hymn books, or at least books of sacred songs, being published. The most famous series of these is that put out between 1625 and 1650 by D.G. Corner. Like their less famous contemporaries, these are mostly music sources; and what they show is a desire on the part of Catholics to make use, in private devotion or para-liturgical services, of the new kind of music which had by then become normal. The tunes tend to be carol-like and innocent. The most famous of these is *'Lasst uns erfreuen'* — the tune which was introduced in Britain by Vaughan Williams in 1906 with the words 'Ye watchers and ye holy ones', and now even more often sung to 'All creatures of our God and King'; this, first appearing in a book published in Cologne in 1623, took its present form, with its chains of Alleluias, as early as 1625. Hymnals nowadays contain other pleasant tunes from sources of this kind, like the carol tune associated with 'He smiles within his cradle'.

The appearance of these tune books indicates that private singing and 'unofficial' singing was probably growing among Catholics, though of course there was no official sanction for the use of these songs in the course of Mass. (That is not to say that they could not be sung, as were some medieval carols, before of after Mass on special festive occasions.) But a much more important development was to follow.

The 17th century was disturbed by much theological controversy and speculation in the Catholic Church, and its official principles of authority were placed under stresses which had not been known before. Everybody knows about the debate with Galileo: but there were comparable internal debates which caused a good deal of anxiety to the officials and indicated a new critical attitude on the part of certain sections of the priesthood and even laity. France was the region most affected by these stresses, and eventually the French hierarchy seems to have sanctioned a measure of liturgical reform. This produced a whole new system of Latin hymnody, and new modern tunes to go with it. Not only do we find a revised Breviary with hymns edited and written by Charles Coffin, Rector of the University of Paris, published in 1736 and representing about fifty years' research; but there also begin to appear local diocesan hymnals each with its own selection of tunes. From these the *English Hymnal* editors collected a number of tunes, all excellent music, which were in that book simply called 'French Church melodies', but which later were mostly traced to their eighteenth-century sources. Among tunes with this kind of origin are 'Christe sanctorum', ('Father we praise thee, now the night is over') and 'Regnator Orbis' or 'O quanta qualia' ('O what their joy and their glory must be'). Here then we have a fine body of hymnody which comes directly out of a movement towards localization and fragmentation within the Catholic Church. The most celebrated of all the tunes we get from this movement is not a 'diocesan' tune but a private one, composed in a French monastery (Douai) but its resident English music copyist, John F. Wade: we sing it to 'O come, all ye faithful', a translation of the Latin words he wrote it for. It is, actually, a most remarkable historical phenomenon, having been written first about 1745, but using the form that just about that time was becoming fashionable among the new English evangelicals — with that repeated phrase in the refrain. Its true origin is, like that of the evangelical tunes, in the popular operatic music of the 1720s and 1730s in England, with which Wade will have been acquainted in his youth.

By the mid-19th century the Catholic authorities reckoned that this private diocesan hymnody had gone far enough, and in the 1870s they put a stop to it. Therefore traditional Catholics are unaware of it, and it would have sunk without trace had not Vaughan Williams imported it for anglican use. After the First Vatican Council (1870), hymnody in the Catholic Church reverted to its former status — either it was written into the liturgy and sung to plainsong, or it was firmly relegated to non-liturgical occasions. But by this time England had entered into the Catholic picture with another form of liturgical dissent.

Throughout Britain since the Reformation the public pursuit of the Roman Catholic religion had been to all intents and purposes illegal. Dispensations were allowed to certain noble families, and in parts of Scotland the interdict proved unenforceable, so that in some regions of the Highlands there are Catholic cultures which have never been disturbed. The part of Ireland which is not part of Great Britain is also an undisturbed Catholic culture. But it was not until 1833 that Roman Catholics were eased of their disabilities, and not until 1850 that their heirarchy was once again set up in Britain.

This re-establishment was, of course, hastened by the Oxford Movement, many of whose leaders joined th Catholic Church. But by 1950 the signs were already abundant that Catholicism, once liberated, would be a very popular culture. In 1849 Frederick William Faber first published his hymns for Catholics, which became so popular as to give English Catholic devotion a colour of its own from the beginning. Faber declared that what Cowper and Newton had done for their parish, he would like to do all for English-speaking Catholics; and although he was no great poet, he had the common touch which at once caused people to delight in such hymns as 'There's a wideness in God's mercy', 'My God, how wonderful thou art', 'O come and mourn with me awhile', 'Hark, hark my soul', and 'Faith of our fathers.' That last one, indeed, was in effect an English Catholic rejoinder to 'A mighty fortress', being quite openly a battle-call to the reconversion of England; the fact that it is immensely popular among American protestants nowadays is ironic enough — but it is balanced by the new experience Catholics allow themselves in including 'A mighty fortress' in their modern hymnals.

Just after 1850 tune books began to appear, containing very easy and sometimes terrifyingly sentimental or monotonous, tunes for congregations to sing to these new hymns, or to the 'Tantum ergo' and 'O Salutaris' which formed the hymnody of that very popular service, Benediction. Benediction in the English form that persisted from 1850 to Vatican II, an evening service in which the congregation is blessed by Christ present in the Blessed Sacrament, was the service which psychologically ministered to the need of people for a devotion that was local, personal, and warm. Probably this association, which above all appealed to the poor who were warmed by a sense of local community and fellowship blessed by the Real Presence, was the reason why Vatican II tended to discourage its continuance; a new attitude to the Mass was designed to provide what Benediction has been giving.

English Catholics in the 19th century were largely Irish immigrants, and they tended to congregate in the large industrial centres and to be conspicuously poor and underprivileged. On the whole Catholicism at that time in England was not so much associated with continental pomp and splendour as with a need to evangelize and comfort the poor: and hymnody like 'Soul of my Saviour' did exactly that. So did the swinging and earthy tunes that became well known.

But the 20th century — we have briefly mentioned this already —produced a new kind of educated and critical Catholic: very good literature came from people like Ronald Knox and G.K. Chesterton and F.J. Sheed: Maurice Baring and Graham Greene led the way in Catholic novel-writing; Richard Terry and Dom Gregory Murray responded by raising standards in Catholic music. It is probably for this reason that when hymnody was liberated by Vatican II — in that Catholics were now positively encouraged to sing hymns at Mass, and were no longer inhibited from singing texts of non-Catholic authorship — the Catholic hymnals tended to reach a high standard. The most interesting are the *New Catholic Hymnal* (1971) and the second edition of *Praise the Lord* (1972); but it is noticeable that both these failed to find a great deal of good new Catholic text-writing. It was too early for that. What they did find was valuable enough — especially Paul Inwood's eloquent and beautiful lyric 'Reap me the earth', and the psalm-versions of Brian Foley. But the standards these editors were enabled to call for were prepared a generation earlier in the *Westminster Hymnal,* second edition, 1940, the only hymnal authorized at the time by the hierarchy for the use of Catholics.

In America the situation has been totally different. English Catholics had the anglican Renaissance behind them and a high tradition of literature and music of their own; and England is a small place. American Catholics are a variegated ethnic mixture: many of them are people whose first language is not English: many of them have no intellectual or critical tradition at all. And America is huge — it is quite impossible for a cultural renaissance of the Dearmer-Vaughan Williams kind to take place in as short a time as it did in Britain. There is probably much more bewilderment among American Catholics than among English ones about the consequences of Vatican II, and there are certainly far more diverse interpretations of it. That is why nothing yet in America corresponds to the best Catholic hymnals in Britain, and why the Catholic communities have been fair game for commercial publishers who have decided what congregations will enjoy and found they were more or less right in putting the standard fairly low.

But the real point is this: that for hymnody to flourish in the Catholic Church a total change has to take place in the Catholic attitude to the church and its worship. Now the change in ethos concerning the Mass, which appeals to many and distresses many others, is a change from the ethos of the ecumenical to that of the local. The worshiping community is now much more of a family. The priest is a quite different kind of being — his turning to face the congregation, though indeed a revival of a very ancient practice, has exactly the effect that the protestant minister's facing the congregation has. Just as with the protestants, the new custom is far more sacerdotal than the old: the priest is not now so much the priest as Father Exe (or not infrequently Henry: not inconceivably, Hank); the encounter in worship becomes a personal encounter, a profoundly different relation from that between an east-facing sacrificial priest and a congregation facing the same way. An emphasis on 'the people of God', the 'church gathered in this place' —familiar in the dissenting protestant traditions and largely now conceded by the anglicans — builds the sheltering walls and provides a context for congregational hymnody.

The only problem is, of course, that this change of focus and ethos strikes many Catholic worshipers as clerically imposed. In all the churches in our time it has been customary for authorities, central committees and working parties of experts to discover what congregations want and do their best to deliver it: not, one would say, the attitude of the medieval curia, and certainly not that of Pope St. Pius X. It has its attractive aspects, of course: but there are plenty of signs that what the commissions claim to have discovered has to some extent been invented, or pressed on them by wholly secular fashions. This is why catholic congregational singing in America has turned out to be so difficult to promote; it is why where it is promoted the promoter feels tempted (and cheerfully yields to the temptation) to use rather vulgar methods to tempt the congregation to sing. And the combination of a frankly protestant ethos of the local congregation with a large ignorance of what the protestants in their classic days did to respond to this in terms of congregational song tends to cause hymn promoters in Catholic churches to flounder. A protestant witness of all this wishes that the Catholics were capable of avoiding the errors made by the English anglicans when they took up hymnody in a big way; such a witness wishes Catholics knew more, or would find out more, about Watts and Wesley and Bridges and Cowper.

Catholic hymn-promoters would be wise to take account of the real size of the problem they have on their hands: and, where the matter in question involves music, to investigate again the techniques of those who have managed in other areas to get congregations to enjoy what is good and simple and innocent and universal. It is, if we may again quote Vaughan Williams, a moral rather than a musical issue: but it may be remembered that 'moral' does not mean merely 'a question of people's bad morals': its basic meaning is simply 'what makes people tick', and this is the question too infrequently asked by promoters of new liturgical customs, including, specifically, hymns at the Catholic Mass.

It is, in fact, not impossible at all to get Catholics singing and enjoying hymns, any more than it is impossible to get congregations to adapt to and enjoy new liturgical forms. But let nobody approach either problem in the spirit, 'Now this is what we're all going to do.' The proper way to approach it is to say, 'now there are perfectly good reasons why people don't want to do this.' There are perfectly good reasons why Catholics initially don't want to sing hymns (or for that matter protestants too); until those who want hymns to adorn Catholic worship have discovered in what conditions, and by the application of what unobtrusive skills, people do want to sing, the present unease will continue, and the Mass will be interrupted and disfigured by hymnody which consists of a strident soloist singing into a microphone against the background of glutinous electronic sound. More particularly: if Catholics want hymn singing at the Mass, they must candidly answer the question whether the change of congregational ethos required to give hymns a good soil to grow in is what the Catholic church really wants: if the answer is anything but 'Yes', then hymns ought to be dropped and left to those Christian groups whose doctrine of congregational worship is founded in the Reformation.

XII

The Main Stream Since 1955

The last two chapters have drawn attention to the confusion and fragmentation of our times, as it has affected the communities for an old tradition, from the Catholic Church to the family. Certainly the effect of these converging storms in the early part of our present age, say 1955-65, was to make hymn writers and editors wonder what they could do, especially if none of the new bandwagons appeared worth jumping on.

One fascinating product of the new confusion and broken communications was the *Cambridge Hymnal* (1967), prompted by the Cambridge University Press as a hymnal for schools, following exactly the line taken by *Songs of Praise* a generation earlier of presenting to school children only what could be approved by their teachers as good music and literature. The difference between it and *Songs of Praise* is that the older book was prepared by people who loved hymns, the younger one by people who were experts in literature and in music (the well known educationist David Holbrook and the excellent and eminent composer Elizabeth Poston). The new team could find only 139 hymns fit for schools — Dearmer had spread himself as far as 703. Standards of professional editing meant nothing to these two enthusiasts, who printed one pair of hymns, on a single page-opening, twice in the book, disdained to check many dates and ascriptions, and concentrated only on excellent music and words: they were further impeded, perhaps, by a conviction that the only good poetry for their purposes was written in the pre-hymn period of the 17th century. The result was a beautiful and idiosyncratic anthology that has nothing really to do with hymnody: and it represents very well the new generation's wish to detach itself from the customs, and even the skills, of the old.

But perhaps the main-stream of traditional hymn writers was saved in England, and to some extent in America, by the new fashion of Hymnal Supplements. In the late 1960s people in both countries were wondering whether the time had not come to revise this or that hymnal; but they always found themselves saying, 'Everything just now is in such a state of flux that we simply don't know what to commit another generation to.' When the editors of the venerable *Hymns Ancient and Modern* said that, the signal was clear. The answer was — keep the old book for a while, but publish an optional Supplement of about a hundred hymns for those who want to move forward.

So in 1969 both the *Hymns Ancient and Modern* and the English Methodists took this line, publishing within weeks of one another *100 Hymns for To-day* and *Hymns and Songs*. The first is what it says it is — a hundred hymns to fill the gaps people felt the 1950 edition of *Hymns Ancient and Modern* had left, and to introduce enough new hymns to indicate what the future policy of the editors might be. *Hymns and Songs* is also accurately titled: the 'hymns', 74 of them, being hymns in conventional style, mostly new, and the 'songs', thirty of them, being experimental material, disposable material, or songs requiring special techniques of singing. Now the great advantage of this method is that you can introduce new things without feeling obliged to discard old things to make room for them. You can commit yourself to the new without making a judgment about the old. So new writers, new composers and new styles get a much better opportunity of exposure, limited only by the fact that the supplement that carries them is one that congregations aren't obliged to buy.

This method was in the end followed by most of the main-line groups in Britain. The Baptists brought out *Praise for To-day* (1974), the United Reformed Church, *New Church Praise* (1975), to serve what until 1972 had been the Congregationalist and Presbyterian congregations of England, and the august imprimatur of the *English Hymnal* lay upon *English Praise* (1976). Informal supplements were brought out by Stainer and Bell, the 'Faith, Folk and Clarity' series, *New Songs for the Church* (1969) and *Songs for the Seventies* (1971) and later, for the Methodist Youth Department, *Partners in Praise* (1979).

In the USA the technique has mostly been followed by the Episcopal Church, which sought to supplement the *Hymnal-1940* first with *More Hymns and Spiritual Songs* (1971), later with a tune-Supplement, *Hymns-II* (1976) and later still with a full Supplement, *Hymns-III* (1979) which heralded the new liturgical emphasis to be followed in a promised full revision. The publication of full-scale hymnals continues in the USA, where economics are not yet as fiercely hostile to such projects as in Britain, and where Christian groups have more confidence in their judgment — or in some cases less capacity for being influenced by anything whatever.

The English Supplements, then, nourished the main stream hymnody of the British tradition, and gave new writers a hearing. Three much sought after hymn writers from England come from the dissenting traditions, Pratt Green from the Methodist, Brian Wren and Fred

Kaan from the Congregational Stream of the United Reformed Church. Pratt Green, after his first appearance in 1969, has at the time of writing (1980) written close on 200 hymns, which are collected in his *Hymns and Ballads* (Hope Publishing Co., 1982). Fred Kaan, of Dutch birth but a minister in England for most of his professional life, has made especially his own the hymn of social conscience and of the modern city: he has a skill with the English language which many natives would envy, and his hymns have travelled farther in a short time than those of any contemporary writer. Wren is strenuously theological and imaginative, again making much of the need for hymns of social conscience, but exploring many varieties of lyric devotion, and of hitherto unexplored theological thought. These, we may say, are in some sense the heirs of Albert Bayly, also from the Congregational tradition, who, a generation older than Kaan or Wren, counts as the first of the new wave of experimental hymn writers, making some of the first gestures towards a hymnody celebrating the scenes, language and special needs of modern urban life.

Among contemporary anglicans in England the most travelled are probably H.C.A. Gaunt, Timothy Dudley-Smith and Michael Hewlett; all of them are on the evangelical side of the centre, and all have written material of sound integrity. The second supplement hymnal of the *Hymns Ancient and Modern* dynasty, *More Hymns for To-day,* introduces two more very promising anglican writers, John E. Bowers and W.H. Vanstone. Our appendix illustrates the work of some of these writers and will confirm our judgement that the writing of hymns on the traditional pattern is by no means a dead art.

What one notices about this new material — and we must attribute this to the shake-up of the fifties — is a new freedom of language and thought; new things need to be said and written about, and the new language, getting rid of 'thou' and substituting 'you' has proved surprisingly fertile in swinging the writers' thoughts into new channels. The same can be said of hymn tunes. My own judgment places the English composer Peter Cutts among the leaders of those who have married new styles with old and accessible thought forms, who, in other words, have written fresh kinds of tune which are immediately singable. His work is best studied in *New Church Praise,* and it will be seen that he is a master of many different musical vocabularies and dialects. But a look at the work of Cyril Taylor, especially in the *BBC Hymn Book* (1951) and in *More Hymns for To-day,* shows how an older composer over forty years has managed to write in many styles, usually with outstanding success.

But perhaps if there is a figure more symbolic than any of these, one would have to say it was the English hymnologist John Wilson. You have to search here and there for his creative work in music because he has never been a prolific composer. Indeed he has written little of any kind. But during a now lengthening lifetime he has stood for honest research, meticulous editing, and the dissemination of good taste with exactly the combination of flexibility and firmness that the times demanded. He has been much in demand as an editorial consultant: *Hymns for Church and School, Hymns and Songs, Hymns for Celebration* (1974), *New Church Praise,* and *Sixteen Hymns of To-day for Use as Simple Anthems* (1978) all owe a certain kind of distinction to his advice or editorship; occasional articles in the Bulletin of the British Hymn Society have corrected and amplified hymnological scholarship (the detail we recorded about the tune *Lasst uns erfreuen* is owed to researches of his published in 1980); and above all his direction of the hymn singing series, *Come and Sing,* which since 1970 has attracted large congregations in Westminster Abbey during the month of May and exposed them to the best in current hymnody, have demonstrated that where one will take the trouble to produce it in a friendly and competent fashion, contemporary hymnody of the best kind will always find friends. *More Hymns for To-day* owes a good deal to him and gives good currency to some of his compositions and arrangements, which have been appearing over a period of nearly fifty years here and there. And if one were to attempt to list the contemporary authors and composers who have writen hymns at his suggestion, or indeed suppressed them at his suggestion, it would be a long one. As a practical scholar-apostle of hymnody he is, at the time of writing, without peer in England, as much an advance on Dearmer as Dearmer was on Helmore.

'Main line hymnody' in America has been less explosive, but at its best no less impressive. The Episcopal *Hymnal-1940* has lasted forty years not least because of the unusual alertness of its editors, and it represents in America a renaissance comparable to that of Dearmer in Britain. The work of three Episcopal writers, all clergy, has continued, and improved on, the good literary work of a hundred years earlier: they are Francis Bland Tucker, Howard Chandler Robbins, and Walter Russell Bowie, all of whom, though not massively productive, have left work of distinction for posterity, and one of whom, Tucker, is still at work in 1980.

But outside the Episcopal church things have moved more slowly; each denomination has produced successive books which tread cautiously in the steps of their predecessors — with the one exception of the *Pilgrim Hymnal.* To-day the most impressive new work has perhaps been done by the Lutherans, a church body with a high sense of professionalism who in their latest book, the *Lutheran Book of Wor-*

ship (1982: designed to be, but not used as, a hymnal uniting the German and Scandinavian traditions of Lutheranism), where one will find unusually lively texts by Martin Franzmann, and some good new music mostly in a neo-German style.

A truly experimental gesture in hymnody was produced in *Ecumenical Praise* (1977), a non-denominational hymn supplement of 117 pieces containing many examples of thoroughly experimental writing: a hymn in "pidgin" English; a piece of electronic tape and voices; an aleatoric set of Alleluias; a clip from the Bernstein Mass; a song by Duke Ellington, alongside texts by Watts and Wesley, tunes by Williamson and Wyton, a Vaughan Williams Magnificat and a good deal of modern hymnody from Sweden, Germany, Africa and India. There is, one supposed in assisting in its editing, room for hymn collections which point towards the 21st century and back their editors' hunches about what that century will want. (The one British hymnal which makes gestures like that is the *Church Hymnary, Third Edition,* 1973, which contains about twenty tunes in a thoroughly futuristic style, none of which should be ignored).

But two things tend to put a brake on the congregational acceptance of new material and their intelligent use of it. One is the enormous success of the choral tradition in church, attributable mainly to the apostleship of John Finley Williamson who founded Westminster Choir College in 1926. To-day so many churches have so many vigorous choral programs that there is normally room only for three hymns in a morning service: and of course there is often no other service in the day, so that a congregation sings about 150 hymns a year, sometimes only 100. The repertory diminishes almost as the square of the diminution of singing opportunities: if you sing few hymns you are the more impatient if any are unfamiliar. Congregational adventurousness in musical matters is declining sharply, even if their taste is very gradually rising.

The other brake is a brake on comprehension produced by the now universal custom of printing hymns as if they were part-songs, with all the text interlined between the music staves. This was always the way in which Gospel Songs were printed, but its effect on the congregation's awareness of the meaning of the words is catastrophic. Consider the following: it is a piece of verse as a congregation sees it in a hymnal:

God him - self is with us: Let us now a - dore him, And with awe ap-
God him - self is with us: Hear the harps re - sound - ing! See the crowds thy
O thou Fount of bles - sing, Pu - ri - fy my spi - rit; Trust - ing on - ly

-pear be - fore him. God is in his tem - ple, All with - in keep
throne sur - round - ing! 'Ho - ly, ho - ly, ho - ly,' hear the hymn as-
in thy mer - it, Like the ho - ly an - gels Who be - hold thy

si - lence, Pros - trate lie with deep - est rev - erence. Him a - lone God we own
cend - ing, An - gels, saints, their voi - ces blend - ing! Bow thine ear To us here:
glo - ry, May I cease - less - ly a - dore three, And in all, Great and small,

Him, our God and Sa - vior; Praise his name for - ev - er.
Hear, O Christ, the prais - es That thy Church now rais - es.
Seek to do most near - ly What thou lov - est dear - ly.

It is not at all surprising that, in encountering the pastors or musicians
whose responsibility it is to choose hymns in worship, one finds total
ignorance of what a hymn is about, and of what bibilical allusions it
contains. It is well known to experts in education that once one has
learned to read at all one reads, not syllables, but blocks of words: one
comprehends the sense by reading phrases. When one is obliged to add
(as I am assured I must by those who know) that the appreciation of
poetry is not now taught in most American schools, then one despairs of
ever being able to share with a congregation the delights and edifica-
tions of singing to music literature whose force and communication
depends on the writer's judgment on the exact sense and weight of
words; and when nobody has seen a poem written out as poetry should
be, the special aids to comprehension afforded by the arrangement of
the lines are entirely lost. The elegant shape of one stanza of the above
hymn is a visual pleasure that importantly aids comprehension of the
stanza's content: thus —

> God himself is with us:
>   let us now adore him,
>   and with awe appear before him.
> God is in his temple,
>   all within keep silence,
>   prostrate lie with deepest reverence.
>   Him alone
>   God we own,
>   him, our God and Savior;
>   praise his name for ever.

Rhyme, metre, phrasing and sense all disappear in the text as currently
printed. Its one advantage is that music readers can pick up a new tune
at once; in fact congregations are not mainly musicians, and because of
that are never asked to do this. An unknown hymn is as inaccessible in
America as it is in an English church were the congregation has words-
books only; and the British device of changing tunes when an alternative in the same metre can be substituted for one that is not familiar, is
almost impossible with the American form of printing.

    The origin of this deplorable custom is in a tendency, not before
1930 shared by all singing bodies, to regard hymns as music with
incidental words: as part songs. Along that road lies the proposition

that so long as you make music it matters little what you sing. Neither the Catholic nor the Protestant historic traditions of hymn singing have ever endorsed so immoral an idea. Along the same road lies also the proposition that whatever is easiest it is best to do: and it remains a truth of human nature that it is at its best when it is called on to do demanding things.

Possibly this tiresome custom is responsible for the fact that American congregations are curiously unwilling to sing tunes in Common Metre or hymns in four short lines. Recently, in attempting to minister to an episcopal congregation, and suggesting that they sing 'The Lord's my Shepherd', which is not in their hymnal, I was faced with the fact that this psalm would have to be sung either to the tune of 'Our God our help in ages past' or to a tune called 'St. Agnes' by J.B. Dykes: no other tune in Common Metre (not even 'Crimond'!) was known to that congregation. And I was told, by a friend who had oversight of the church music throughout the churches of a certain denomination in one of the American states, that 'they won't sing two-line hymns.' This meant that hymns occupying only two musical systems on a page were ostracized in favour of hymns that occupied four: which gave 'Blessed assurance' the edge over 'Our God, our help in ages past.' This is another weird product of the custom of interlining words — justifiable, surely, only where the text is so irregular that there might be doubt where the words fitted into the tune: there are three or four hymns in the repertory that are like that.

And the custom is certainly responsible for the kind of thing one sees when for some reason a text has to be extracted from its music scores and printed in a service paper. This is what can happen (I can testify that it has happened):

> I love thy kingdom, Lord, the house of
> thine abode, the Church our blest Re-
> deemer saved with his most precious blood.

> For her my tears shall fall, for her my
> prayers ascend; to her my cares and
> toils be given 'till cares and toils shall end.
>
> . . . and so on.

In honesty I must add that whenever I have made this point in public I have been savaged by the musicians, and never defended by even unmusical pastors: so it looks like a battle that will not for a long time, if ever, be even joined, let alone won.

One other matter must be mentioned which is having an effect, not at present very encouraging, on the writing of contemporary hymns in America, and is likely to have the same effect in England. This is a peculiar preoccupation with language which in America has filled the void left by the disappearance of an interest in style or in poetry.

Two streams are running here. One is the familiar liturgical stream which has insisted that language used in worship shall be 'modern' or 'contemporary.' This has produced a shelf-full of new versions of the Bible, and a new liturgical speech which is now accepted by all the major denominations in both countries. This is not the place to discuss the liturgical implications of this: we only note it, and say that it has proved to be a stick with two ends when it has affected hymnody. On the one hand, the hymn writers we mentioned earlier have shown that one can write naturally and gracefully in a language which does not affect the cadences and inflections of seventeenth century English. The translators of the New English Bible Apocrypha (more than those of the Old and New Testaments) have shown that it is possible to write a commanding and eloquent translation of an ancient original in modern speech. And good liturgists like Canon Poole, from 1958 to 1977 Precentor of Coventry Cathedral, have shown that liturgical language need not be clumsy or crude if it is such as falls naturally on modern ears.

But the stick points the other way also; the demand for new language has encouraged some writers to attempt it who can't write — who have no ear for rhythm and who have an insufficiently developed sensitiveness to the precise meaning of words. The official new liturgies are not quite free of this taint: some liturgical utterances of less wide distribution are seriously disfigured by it. I venture to quote once again what I quoted in an earlier book now out of print. I was asking a young candidate for church membership, aged about fifteen, what her Bible reading habits were and whether she had by any chance looked at the New English Bible, New Testament, which had recently appeared. 'Yes, I have', she said; 'it doesn't make it any easier.' In which moment she lifted up her voice and prophesied. If new language is designed to please those who want it made easier, that design and purpose are corrupt and wrong. Faithfulness to the truth is one thing: the shaving off of its asperities and the papering over of its difficulties is quite another. New English Bible *Romans* should be approached with the expectation that it will show where the difficulties, and the genius, of Romans really lie. Romans 5. 1-15, for example is difficult in King James because the English adds difficulties to the Greek; a new translation may well expose the meaning of the original quite lucidly, but if anyone thinks that this is going to make Paul's thought less demanding, disappointment is assuredly in store.

The coming of new language into worship has encouraged some writers to write what sounds modern but what also offends the decencies of grammar and syntax: deceived into thinking you can translate the old language into the new, writer after writer of prayers and hymns replaced 'O thou who givest' by 'O you who gives.' (The recent Canadian *Hymn Book* of 1971 is a bad offender in this respect, and when I remonstrated about this with a friend the answer was that there were two professors of English on its committee who said it didn't matter.) Modern language must never be thought of as a short cut to instant comprehension, or to instant poetry: it's no easier to handle than King James English. But at least we can say that people are handling it very well in many places.

The same cannot quite be said of the other stream of modernization, which comes from those who wish to remove from liturgical language (indeed from all speech and writing) the turns of phrase which they describe as 'sexist.' Since I have written elsewhere about this,* I will here only say that it is the only example I know of in history where an attempt has been made to reconstruct a living language in the interests of a pressure group. My interim conclusions about this can be summed up in the proposition that the casual use of non-generic words like 'man' for 'humanity' can often be adjusted, and should perhaps be avoided in modern speech, whereas the elimination of any reference to God in the male gender is a theological reconstruction with which I simply doubt whether the proposers are competent to deal. Since so eminent a practitioner of hymn writing as Brian Wren has espoused this cause in Britain, I admit that I feel unsure of my ground if I say that theology cannot be so reconstructed: but a time when the case against 'sexist language' is being put with so much passion, anger and occasionally deliberate unkindness and discourtesy seems to be inappropriate for so delicate and responsible an operation as the changing of theological language.

However that may be, the pressure of this group has caused a good deal of clumsy adaptation of older texts; and as with the liturgies, what has appeared in hymnals. such as the *Lutheran Book of Worship,* is nothing to what is often done locally. When such pressures result in the abandonment of precision and delicacy in speech or writing, it is attacking a principle of civilized living which we dare not allow to go undefended. The proponents of this fashion behave with texts as the eighteenth century evangelicals behaved with music — producing rather often caricatures of the original which, had they been submitted to public judgment in that form at first, would never have come into currency at all.

Worship Magazine, Vol. 53 #1, January 1979: *The Hymn,* January 1980 (the same article reprinted): and *Worship* Vol. 56 #3, March 1982.

These things have given pause to hymn writers of sensitiveness; the best advice to give such writers is to cast their work in a form which will not be needlessly antiquated and will not arouse legitimate criticism on the grounds of using non-inclusive language when it is humanity that is being referred to. Beyond that I think it unwise to go.

XIII
Whither from Here?

Much has had to be omitted, and much only sketchily referred to, in these pages; but I hope the central point has been made, which is that the congregational singing of hymns is not by any means the universal or historically assumable thing that we often think it is. We have referred to cultures in which hymns are largely solos, and others in which they were mostly choral; and we have noted that the kind of congregational singing which we now assume people should aim at is nourished by a sense of community, by the existence or the formation of an identifiable group, marked off from the rest of the world by tradition, or protest, or charismatic leadership, or a mixture of all three.

The fact is that congregational singing as we know it is the end-product of a long process. In that process the idea of congregational singing caught on faster in some communities than in others. It is quite obvious that when Dearmer and Vaughan Williams and Martin Shaw crusaded for better congregational singing in the parishes they had encountered a situation in which congregational singing was by no means assumed; oddly enough all three of them, at the beginning of their crusade, knew precious little about those non-anglican protestant churches in which congregational singing was hearty, resourceful and convinced: but it was their technique which they were adapting for the anglicans. And it has to be their technique which in these latter days has, in some way, to be sold to the Catholics.

We have seen that the most effective and fervent hymn singing comes from the fringes of the church rather than from its historic Catholic center. Nowadays the smaller the body, the less problem there is about congregational singing — as with the Mennonites and the Moravians. The largest body of all is finding the problems most acute.

Well now: let us finally ask the question why C.S. Lewis hated hymns so much. He is only the most famous of a quite large number of learned people, who were also devout Christians, to whom hymns were repellent. He often said and wrote that he disliked hymns, and never in so many words told us exactly why. But at two points he did, I think, give us clues to his dislike of them.

103

The first is where in the *Screwtape Letters* he described hymns as 'the corrupt texts of second-rate lyrics.' As a scholar in the English language, and a master of its precise use, he found offensive the editors' customs of altering any writer's original. Of course, he was totally unimpressed (for reasons we are about to mention) by the folk-song status of hymns, and by the fact that when one writes a hymn or tune one has let it loose among people who bring to it the judgment of the unliterary and the unmusical, and whose judgment is not always to be despised. These people are not usually editors but ordinary members of congregations: and since they are using both poetry and music as aids to a further purpose, and not as objects of study in their own right, it is not in fact thought improper if an editor alters 'bowels' to 'mercies' in a Charles Wesley hymn. Fair enough. But that is not quite the whole story: for while such adjustments are not always frowned on in hymn singing, they can, obviously, be the result of a casual, insensitive and imprecise approach to things, of a longing for ease and short cuts to religious experience, which is one of the things a disciplined mind like Lewis's detested most. He was right to detest it. The fatal ease with which hasty Christians confuse compassion and casualness is one of the most disagreeable things about them.

But for more light on this one should turn to his essay, 'The Inner Ring' (*They Asked for a Paper*, 1962, pp 139ff). This is not only an essay in the loftiest traditions of its author's perspicacity and moral shrewdness: it is also one of the few really revealing personal documents he left. His subject is the existence, and the required attitude towards, those unofficial caucuses, gangs, groups of friends, or 'Inner Rings', which exist within any hierarchical system and are quite independent of it. Consider any group of people who seem often to gather together, but of whom you are not one: focus on such a group when it promotes decisions of a general kind which will bear on yourself: have in mind the sense of 'being left out' which one feels in the presence of such a ring — of people as it were whose backs are always towards you — and the peculiar resentment which you feel if you are not part of it. Then consider (he says) the singular joy of being invited in. Consider, he goes on, what you would be prepared to pay for that pleasure. Consider, he further says, how many pay dearly.

> It would be polite and charitable, and in view of your age reasonable too, to suppose that none of you is yet a scoundrel. On the other hand, by the mere law of averages (I am saying nothing against free will) it is almost certain that at least two or three of you before you die will have become something very like scoundrels. There must be in this room the makings of at least that

number of unscrupulous, treacherous, ruthless egotists. The choice is still before you: and I hope you will not take my hard words about your possible future characters as a token of disrepsect to your present characters. And the prophecy I make is this. To nine out of ten of you the choice which could lead to scoundrelism will come, when it does come, in no very dramatic colours. Obviously bad men, obviously threatening or bribing, will almost certainly not appear. Over a drink or a cup of coffee, disguised as a triviality and sandwiched between two jokes, from the lips of a man or a woman whom you have recently been getting to know rather better and whom you hope to know better still — just at the moment when you are most anxious not to apear crude, or naif or a prig — the hint will come. It will be the hint of something which is not quite in accordance with the technical rules of fair play: something which the public, the ignorant, romantic public, would never understand: something which even the outsiders in your own profession are apt to make a fuss about: but something, says your new friend, which 'we' — and at that word 'we' you try not to blush for mere pleasure — something 'we always do.' And you will be drawn in, if you are drawn in, not by desire for gain or ease, but simply because you cannot bear to be thrust back into the cold outer world. It would be so terrible to see the other man's face —that genial, confidential, delightfully sophisticated face — turn suddenly cold and contemptuous, to know that you had been tried for the Inner Ring and rejected. And then, if you are drawn in, next week it will be something a little further from the rules, and next year something further still, but all in the jolliest, friendliest spirit. It may end in a crash, a scandal, and penal servitude: it may end in millions, a peerage and giving the prizes at your old school. But you will be a scoundrel...... Of all passions the passion for the Inner Ring is most skilful in making a man who is not yet a very bad man do very bad things.

That was originally an address delivered to students at King's College, London in 1944. Its relevance to our study is this. Lewis uses here and throughout his address the fruit of much personal experience to give a salutary moral warning. He was, as his autobiography shows, a person peculiarly vulnerable to the atmosphere generated by gangs, or caucuses, or inner rings of hearty and sociable people. One beomes most conscious of this climate if one is educated at a residential English school — which Lewis was, and which he loathed. He admits that 'inner rings' are inevitable in society but he discloses, in his passionate denunciation of them (and the point he makes above is a perfectly valid one) a nature sensitive to their effects on the shy and inarticulate who lack self-confidence.

Lewis hated hymns because he heard them as the church's gang-songs. A crowd-hater and crowd-fearer if ever there was one, his idea of worship was not the packed church fastening on the words of a star preacher (ironically enough nobody in the 1940s could be so surely guaranteed to pack a church or any other building as Lewis) but a contemplative act in the presence of a few. Lewis would probably have had no use for the modern tendency to see worship as the celebration of a local church's corporateness. But most certainly he thought the singing church was the church at its most repulsive.

He was, of course, saying what we have been saying in this book, but putting a cutting edge on it. The very nature of hymnody, we have insisted is local: it thrives in the identifiable community, and you can always think of that community as an inner ring. You can go further. You can go quite as far as Lewis goes when he points out the temptation that acts on the insecure person to get into a ring and to respond with joy to an invitation to join it: and when he goes on from there to say that that is how many criminals are made. Indeed, some forms of the singing church turn out to be not far from scoundrelly. Hymn singing can induce a boisterous insensitiveness, a contempt for the non-conforming and the solitary, an exaltation of the group over the individual of the kind in which any tyrant or Komissar takes satisfaction. If nations can be persuaded to be warlike by songs, churches can be persuaded to be 'unscrupulous, treacherous and ruthlessly egotistic'; and to be sure, when Lewis pours scorn on the corrupt texts and the second rate lyrics, they symbolize for him the callous discourtesy and inconsiderateness which plenty of zealous Christians feel licensed by their evangelical ardour to display.

Thirty years ago I wrote as the opening words of a book about hymns that those who found the hymns of the church repulsive must be always reckoned with. I could not write a page until I have got that off my chest (*Hymns and Human Life,* 1951); the passing of years has not dimmed my love for hymns nor altered or diminished my sense that they are dangerous things. At the end of that same book I gave a few examples of bad or ridiculous hymns, which I think provided readers with a little entertainment. That I would not now do. For every point of danger in bad writing or bad composing I would award ten points of danger for bad use, bad choice, casual and insensitive attitudes towards hymns. And I would award a hundred for the unscrupulous use of them to soften up people and silence their criticism of what their local leaders want them to believe.

Hymns, like all degenerate art, can encourage the slothful to remain slothful, the ignorant to stay ignorant, the malicious to take pride in being malicious. They can replace faith by complacency and love by sentimentality. But where a hymn in a service of worship beckons to the worshiper at his or her best and causes that worshiper to feel or say, 'That is what I wanted to say, but I am grateful to whoever put the words in my mouth,' then it has done its work. Hymns can stunt the growth and frustrate the pilgrimage of Christian souls: but they can also nourish and fortify. The same hymns, misused, can do damage, and rightly used, can do good. Some hymns edify one generation and miss the target with another; some, forgotten in their own generation, come to life two hundred years later.

So those who write and compose hymns, those who edit the hymnals, and those who appoint them for worship and play and sing them are a team engaged in a business which no Christian age, and few religions of any kind, have regarded as irrelevant or unnecessary. Singing goes with whatever means most to people. But hymnody introduces into the life of the church a creative tension between the passing and the timeless, between the spatially universal and the local, which without them the church would disregard to its lasting detriment. It is neither unexpected nor inappropriate that so much controversy gathers round them, and so many adventures happen to them. It is perhaps surprising rather how much abuse they survive: but, if we may ignore for a moment the present age's impatience with history, we may judge that what meant so much to Ambrose, St. Francis and St. Thomas Aquinas, to J.S. Bach and Isaac Watts and John Wesley, to Vaughan Williams, Benjamin Britten and your own Christian neighbour, is worth treasuring, preserving and nourishing. Even if our heathen children don't want them, we will not hide them from them: another generation will be grateful if we don't.

APPENDIX

A small cluster of contemporary hymns (none of which is in the *Panorama*)

1

Albert Bayly, b. 1901

Lord of the boundless curves of space
and time's deep mystery,
to your creative might we trace
all nature's energy.

Your mind conceived the galaxy,
each atom's secret planned,
and every age of history
your purpose, Lord, has planned.

Your Spirit gave the living cell
its hidden, vital force;
the instincts which all life impel
derive from you, their Source.

Yours is the image stamped on man,
though marred by man's own sin;
and yours the liberating plan
again his soul to win.

Science explores your reason's ways,
and faith can this impart
that in the face of Christ our gaze
looks deep within your heart.

Christ is your wisdom's perfect word,
your mercy's crowning deed:
in him the sons of earth have heard
your strong compassion plead.

Give us to know your truth; but more,
the strength to do your will;
until the love our souls adore
shall all our being fill.

2

Frederick Pratt Green, b. 1903

To mock your reign, O dearest Lord,
they made a crown of thorns;
set you with taunts along the road
from which no man returns.
They could not know, as we do now,
how glorious is that crown,
that thorns would flower upon your brow,
your sorrows heal our own.

In mock acclaim, O gracious Lord,
the snatched a purple cloak,
your passion turned, for all they cared
into a soldier's joke.
They could not know, as we do now,
that though we merit blame
you will your robe of mercy throw
around our naked shame.

A sceptred reed, O patient Lord,
they thrust into your hand,
and acted out their grim charade
to its appointed end.
They could not know, as we do now,
though empires rise and fall,
your Kingdom shall not cease to grow
till love embraces all.

(1978)

109

3

W. H. Vanstone, b. 1923

Morning glory, starlit sky,
    soaring music, scholar's truth,
flight of swallows, autumn leaves,
    memory's treasure, grace of youth:

open are the gifts of God,
    gifts of love to mind and sense,
hidden is love's agony,
    love's endeavour, love's expense.

Love that gives, gives evermore,
    gives with zeal, with eager hands,
spares not, leaps not, all outpours,
    ventures all, its all expands.

Drained is love in making full,
    bound in setting others free,
poor in making many rich,
    weak in giving power to be.

Therefore he who shows us God
    and helpless hangs upon the Tree;
and the nails and crown of thorns
    tell of what God's love must be.

Here is God: no monarch he
    throned in easy state to reign;
here is God, whose arms of love,
    aching, spent, the world sustain.

(1977)

4

Timothy Dudley-Smith, b. 1926

Christ be my leader by night as by day,
safe through the darkness, for he is the way.
Gladly I follow, my future his care,
darkness is daylight when Jesus is there.

Christ be my teacher in age as in youth,
drifting or doubting, for he is the truth.
Grant me to trust him; though shifting as sand,
doubt cannot daunt me; in Jesus I stand.

Christ be my Saviour, in calm as in strife;
death cannot hold me, for he is the life.
Not darkness nor doubting nor sin and its stain
can touch my salvation; with Jesus I reign.

5

Brian Wren, b. 1936

Lord God, your love has called us here
    as we, by love, for love were made.
Your living likeness still we bear,
    though marred, dishonoured, disobeyed.
We come, with all our heart and mind
your call to hear, your love to find.

We come with self-inflicted pains
    of broken trust and chosen wrong,
half-free, half-bound by inner chains,
    by social forces swept along,
by powers and systems close confined
yet seeking hope for lost mankind.

Lord God, in Christ you call our name
    and then receive us as your own
not through some merit, right or claim
    but by your gracious love alone.
We strain to glimpse your mercy-seat
and find you kneeling at our feet.

Then take the towel, and break the bread
    and humble us, and call us friends.
Suffer and serve till all are fed,
    and show how grandly love intends
to work till all creation sings,
to fill all worlds, to crown all things.

Lord God, in Christ you set us free
    your life to live, your joy to share.
Give us your Spirit's Liberty
    to turn from guilt and dull despair
and offer all that faith can do
while love is making all things new.

(1973)

6

Fred Kaan, b. 1929

Now join we, to praise the Creator,
   our voices in worship and song;
we stand to recall with thanksgiving
   that to him all seasons belong.

We thank you, O God, for your goodness,
   for the joy and abundance of crops,
for food that is stored in our larders,
   for all we can buy in the shops.

But also of need and starvation
   we sing with concern and despair,
of skills that are used for destruction,
   of land that is burnt and laid bare.

We cry for the plight of the hungry
   while harvests are left on the field,
for orchards neglected and wasting,
   for produce from markets withheld.

The song grows in depth and in wideness:
   the earth and its people are one.
There can be no thanks without giving,
   no words without deeds that are done.

Then teach us, O Lord of the harvest,
   to be humble in all that we claim;
to share what we have with the nations,
   to care for the world in your name.

(1968)

7

(American)

Francis Bland Tucker, b. 1895

O Christ our Savior, who must reign
   till all the world is yours,
let all men hear the joyful strain
   the heavenly host outpours.
Your praise now makes your people one,
   of many a name and birth;
the song in Bethlehem begun
   is hope for all the earth.

Your Gospel to the nations take,
   that you for all have died,
for only gratitude can break
   man's stubbornness and pride.
Your grace alone can conquer hate,
   can turn us to your ways,
and of our thankfulness create
   the fellowship of praise.

Go forth, O Christ, to victory
   by God's eternal plan,
till all shall come in unity
   unto the perfect man;
till rooted, grounded in that love
   for us once sacrificed
your Christ attain the measure of
   the fulness of the Christ.

(1971)

8

Martin Franzmann, 1907-76

In Adam we have all been one,
   one huge rebellious man;
we all have fled that evening voice
   that sought us as we ran.

We fled thee, and in losing thee
   we lost our brother too;
each singly sought and claimed his own;
   each man his brother slew.

But thy strong love, it sought us still
   and sent thine only Son
that we might hear his shepherd's voice
   and, hearing him, be one.

O thou, who, when we loved thee not,
   didst love and save us all;
thou great good Shepherd of mankind,
   oh, hear us when we call.

Send us thy Spirit, teach us truth:
   thou Son, oh, set us free
from fancied wisdom, self-sought ways,
   and make us one in thee.

Then shall our songs united rise
   to thine eternal throne;
where with the Father evermore
   and Spirit, thou art one.

(1969)

9

Jaroslav Vajda, b. 1919

Up through endless ranks of angels,
　　cries of triumph in his ears.
To his heavenly throne ascending,
　　having vanquished all their fears,
Christ looks down upon his faithful,
　　leaving them in happy tears.

Death-destroying, life-restoring,
　　proven equal to our need,
now for us before the Father,
　　as our brother intercede;
flesh that for our world was wounded,
　　living, for the wounded plead!

To our lives of wanton wandering
　　send your promised Spirit-Guide;
through our lives of fear and failure
　　with your power and love abide;
welcome us, as you were welcomed
　　to an endless Eastertide.

Alleluia! Alleluia!
　　oh, to breathe the Sprit's grace!
Allelluia! Alleluia!
　　oh, to see the Father's face!
Alleluia! Alleluia!
　　oh, to feel the Son's embrace!

(1978)

10

William Gay, b. 1920

Each winter as the year grows older,
　　a man grows older too.
The chill sets in a little colder;
　　the verities I knew
　　seem shaken and untrue.

When race and class cry out for treason,
　　when sirens call for war,
they overshout the voice of reason
　　and scream till we ignore
　　all we held dear before.

But I believe beyond believing
　　that life can spring from death;
that growth can flower from our grieving;
　　that man can catch his breath
　　and turn transfixed by faith.

So even as the sun is turning
　　to journey to the north,
the living flame, in secret burning
　　can kindle on the earth,
　　and bring God's love to birth.

O Child of ecstasy and sorrows,
　　O Prince of peace and pain,
brighten to-day's world by to-morrow's,
　　renew our lives again;
　　Lord Jesus, come and reign!

(1975)

11

Catherine Cameron, b. 1927

God, who stretched the spangled heavens,
　　infinite in time and place,
flung the suns in burning radiance
　　through the silent fields of space.
We, thy children, in thy likeness,
　　share inventive powers with thee;
great Creator, still creating,
　　teach us what we yet may be.

Proudly rise our modern cities,
　　stately buildings, row on row;
yet their windows, blank, unfeeling
　　stare on canyoned streets below
where the lonely drift unnoticed
　　in the city's ebb and flow,
lost to purpose and to meaning,
　　scarcely caring where they go.

We have conquered worlds undreamed-of
　　since the childhood of our race;
known the ecstasy of winging
　　through uncharted realms of space,
probed the secrets of the atom,
　　yielding unimagined power,
facing us with life's destruction,
　　or our most triumphant hour.

As thy new horizons beckon,
　　Father, give us strength to be
children of creative purpose,
　　thinking thy thoughts after thee,
till our dreams are rich with meaning,
　　each endeavor, thy design:
great Creator, lead us onward
　　till our work is one with Thine.

(1979)

SOURCES AND ACKNOWLEDGEMENTS.

1. *New Church Praise* 60: *More Hyumns for To-day* 160 from *Rejoice, O People,* 1950: copyright Oxford University Press, London. By permission.

2. *Sixteen Hymns* (ed. John Wilson, RSCM 1978) #8: Songs of Thanks & Praise (Hinshaw 1980) 31. Copyright Hope Publishing Co. By permission.

3. *More Hymns for To-day* (1980) 163. Copyright J.W. Shore. By permission.

4. *Grace Hymns* (1977) 729. Copyright the Rt. Rev. Timothy Dudley Smith, Bishop of Thetford. By permission.

5. *New Church Praise* (1957) 57: from *Mainly Hymns* (1980). Copyright Oxford University Press, London. By permission.

6. *New Catholic Hymnal* (1971) 170: *New Chruch Praise* 71: *Westminster Praise* 17 From Pilgrim Praise (1971). Copyright Stainer & Bell, by permission.

7. *More Hymns and Spiritual Songs* 43, Copyright Walton Music Corp. By permission.

8. *Worship Supplement (1969) 759: Lutheran Book of Worship 372. Copyright Concordia Publishing House. By permission.*

9. *Lutheran Book of Worship 159. Copyright Augsburg Publishing House.* By permission.

10. *United Church of Christ Hymnal* 122. From *A New Song 3,* 1971, Copyright United Church Press. By permission.

11. *Ecumenical Praise* 81: altd, *Lutheran Book of Worship* 463. Copyright 1971 Catherine Cameron. By permission.

— — — — — —

No. 2 was written for the tune TALLIS III
No. 5 was written for the tune ABINGDON

— — — — — —

INDEX OF HYMNS

This is for the convenience of readers who wish to look at the full text or tune of a hymn mentioned in the book.

The hymns appear in the order in which they appear in the book: but readers should note that sometimes a hymn appears in different versions or translations from book to book, and this makes a first line not exactly the same as what is mentioned in our pages: or sometimes a hymn begins in one book with a different stanza from that quoted. But the hymn will usually be recognizable.

The abbreviations stand for the following books:

American

B   — *Baptist Hymnal*, 1975, Broadman Press, Nashville TN

H   — *The Hymnal 1940*, Church Hymnal Corporation, New York

H*   (below 100) *More Hymns and Spiritual Songs*, Walton Music Corp., New York;

     (above 100) Hymns — III, 1978, Church Hymnal Corporation

L   — *Lutheran Book of Worship*, 1978, Augsburg and Concordia

M   — *Methodist Hymnal*, 1964, 1966, Abingdon, Nashville TN

P   — *The Hymnbook*, 1955 (Presbyterian), Westminster Press, Philadelphia

Pm — *Pilgrim Hymnal*, 1958, Pilgrim Press, New York

English

A   — *Hymns Ancient and Modern*, Revised 1950, London, Clowes Ltd.

A*   (below 100) 100 Hymns for To-day (above 100) *More Hymns for To-day*, Clowes

E   — *English Hymnal*, 1906, Oxford University Press

E*   *English Praise*, 1976

C   — *Congregational Praise*, 1951, Independent Press

C*   *New Church Praise*, 1975, Edinburgh, St. Andrew Press

M   — *Methodist Hymn Book*, 1933, Methodist Publishing House

M*   *Hymns and Songs*, 1969, Methodist Publishing House

	Baptist Hymnal 75	Hymnal-1940	Lutheran Book of Worship 78	Methodist Hymnal 64	Presbyterian 55 *Worshipbook 72	Pilgrim Hymnal 58	Hymns A & M 1950 *100 Hymns for Today More Hymns for To-day	English Hymnal *English Praise	Congregational Praise *New Church Praise	Methodist Hymn Book *Hymns and Songs
		AMERICAN					BRITISH			
8 O gladsome light		176	(279)		61		269	611		
8 Hail gladdening light							18		612	937
9 Father we thank thee who hast planted		195		307		289	24*	62*	16*	
9 The great Creator of the worlds		298					178*			
9 All praise to thee	43	366		74		147	4*		197	2*
9 Deus creator omnium (tr.)								49		
9 The eternal gifts of Christ		132					503	175		
10 Now that the daylight		159	268				1	254		
10 Before the ending		164	277				16	276		
10 The glory of these forty days		61						68		
10 Ye choirs of new Jerusalem								122		
11 Christ is made the sure foundation		384	367	298	433	263	620	170	237	7*
11 Of the Father's love begotten	62	20	42	357	7	111	591	613	76	83
11 All glory laud and honor	39	62	108	424	187		598	622	120	84
11 Sing my tongue the glorious battle		66	118				97	95	125	
11 The royal banners		63	125				96	94	126	184
11 Christians to the Paschal Victim		97	137				138	130		
11 Dies Irae (tr)		468					466	351		
11 Jesu the very thought of thee	73	462	316	82	401	226	189	419	173	108
11 Jerusalem the golden		597	347	303	428	309	278	412	352	652
12 Orientis partibus (tune)		H59	130	162			524	129	34	87
12 Come down, O love divine		376	508	466		239	235	152	204	273
13 O what their joy		589	337		424	310	281	465	349	
13 Alone thou goest forth		68		427		159				
13 Of the glorious body telling (Pange lingua)		199					383	326		63*
13 Laud, O Zion, thy salvation		193					622	317		
13 The word of God (O salutaris)		209					384	330		
13 Come ye faithful raise the strain		94	132	448	205	186	133	131	140	
13 The day of resurrection		96	141	437	208		132	137	141	208
13 Let all mortal flesh keep silence		197	198	324	148	107	390	318		38*
16 All glory be to God on high		190	166		283*					
16 In one true God we all believe			374							
16 A mighty fortress (A safe stronghold)	37	551	229	20	91	363	183	362	485	494
16 From heaven above to you I come		22	51						78	126
16 Christ Jesus lay in death's		H62	134	438					761	210

	B	H	L	M	P	Pm	A	E	C	M
16 Savior of the Gentiles			28		565*					
17 Out of the depths (Ps. 130)			295	526					381	359
18 NUN FREUT EUCH 1524			299					148		
18 NUN FREUT EUCH 1535			321	58	16	271	366²	4	520	71
40 ES IST DAS HEIL			194				366¹	478		
18 Sleepers wake		3	31	366		108	55	12	760	255
18 How brightly gleams (O morning star)		329	43	399	415	145		10*		33*
19 Christ the Lord is risen again	1	129*					136	129	142	207
19 MIT FREUDEN ZART	206	522		4	15	20	423	604		415
20 NUNC DIMITTIS		176			61	49		269	611	
20 DONNE SECOURS (Ps. 12)			493		285	398	5	564	116	
20 PSALM 42 (Freu dich sehr)	77	103*	29			104	523	200		
20 PSALM 68 (Old 113th)				9	558*			544	713	584
20 PSALM 86							514	640	383	
20 PSALM 118 (Rendez a Dieu)		195		323		289	409	305	303	756
20 PSALM 124 (Old 124th)		536	376	475	357	451	381	115	586	912
20 PSALM 130							252	254		
20 PSALM 134 (Old 100th)	17	278	245	21	24	4	166	365	1	2
20 COMMANDMENTS		179		307			554	277	626	667
24 Come, Holy Ghost, our souls inspire		217	472	467	237	575	157	153	199	779
24 FOREST GREEN	154	21		33	485		65	15	113	897
57 PSALM 107			318	468	403*			443	53	
26 WINCHESTER OLD	96	13	264	54	381	146	62	30	80	129
26 WINDSOR		284	114	428		226	334	332		237
26 DUNDEE	439	497	464	215	112	389	80	43	361	625
29 When I survey the wondrous cross	111	337	482	435	198	177	108	107	131	182
30 Jesus shall reign	282	542	530	472	496	202	220	420	158	272
30 Our God, our help	223	289	320	28	111	1	165	450	52	878
36 O sacred head	105	75	116	418	194	170	111	102	127	202
36 All my heart this night rejoices		32	46	379	172	123			81	121
36 Commit thou all thy griefs										
(Give to the winds thy fears)	224	(446)		51	364	338			487	507
36 Deck thyself my soul (Schmücke dich)		210	224	318			306	393	293	
36 Jesus still lead on (guide our way)	500		341		334		206		490	624
38 Now I have found the ground									468	375
38 All my hope on God is founded		188*				339	3*	73*	417	70
38 O God my faithful God			504							
39 Lo, he comes		5	27	364	234		51	7	160	264
39 Hark the herald angels	83	27	60	388	163	120	60	24	84	117
39 Christ the Lord is risen today	114		130	439		182	(141)	(160)	145	204
39 Hail the day that sees him rise		104				205	147	143	154	221
39 Love divine	58	479	315	283	399	228	205	437	179	431

	B	H	L	M	P	Pm	A	E	C	M
39 Christ whose glory fills		153	265	401	47	43	7	258	594	924
39 Forth in thy name		150	505	152		406	336	259	593	590
39 Rejoice the Lord is King	120	350	171	483	140	204	216	476	161	247
40 Come O thou Traveller				529			343	378	495	339
45 Come thou Fount of every blessing	13		499	93	379				442	417
45 O God of Bethel		497			342	389	299	447	55	607
45 Hark the glad sound		7	35		410*		53	6	74	82
45 All hail the power	42	355	328	72	132	195	217	364	163	91
45 The God of Abraham	25	285	544		(89)	(14)	631	646	12	21
45 Praise the Lord: ye heavens	11	228*	540	42	3	13	368	535	13	13
45 Spirit of mercy		111					153	631		
46 Guide me, O thou great Jehovah	202	205*	343	271	339	93	296	397	500	615
46 God moves in a mysterious way	439	310	483	215	112	85	181	394	56	503
46 Sometimes a light surprises	221	443		231	418		176		398	527
46 Hark, my soul, it is the Lord		459			263		344	400	374	432
46 O for a closer walk		416		268	319	349	326	445	476	461
46 How sweet the name of Jesus sounds	464	455	345	81	130	221	192	405	182	99
46 Glorious things of thee		385	358	293	437	267	257	393	243	706
46 Amazing grace	165		448	92	275					
46 What various hindrances							246†			
47 Begone unbelief									396	511
47 The spacious firmament		309		43	97	72	170	297	30	44
47 When all thy mercies	468	297	264	70	119	94	177	511	49	413
48 O God of Bethel		497			342	389	299	447	55	607
48 Come let us to the Lord our God					125				386	342
48 The race that long in darkness				(361)	153		(80)	43	75	139
49 The Lord's my Shepherd	341	237*	451	68	104	84	93*	80*	729	50
49 Creator Spirit by whose aid								156	200	293
49 Rise, crowned with light!		389								
49 Hail to the Lord's Anointed		545	87	359	146	105	219	45	326	245
49 O Spirit of the living God		256	388	/	242	299			323	
49 Stand up and bless the Lord	26			16		25	374	90*	270	685
49 Lift up your heads ye gates of brass							306	549	324	265
49 God is our strong salvation	343			211	347	373			501	
49 Christians awake		16				127	61	21	82	120
49 O thou from whom all goodness flows							117	85	766	
49 Jerusalem my happy home	488						282		353	650
50 Prayer is the soul's sincere desire	400	419		252	391	(336)		474	(445)	533
51 Brightest and best		46	84	400	175	126	75	41	94	122
51 Bread of the world		196		323	445	282	409	305	303	759
51 Holy Holy Holy	1	266	165	26	11	251	160	162	223	36
51 O worship the King	30	288	548	473	26	6	167	466	17	8

†: Standard edition, 1922

	B	H	L	M	P	Pm	A	E	C	M
51 Praise my soul	8	282	549	66	31	16	365	470	18	12
51 New every morning		155		499	45	36	4	260	596	(927)
51 Sun of my soul		166		502	56	50	24	274	621	942
51 Ride on! ride on in majesty		64	121	425	188	176	99	620	122	192
51 Schmücke dich		210	224	318			306	393	293	
51 Eternal light!		478							21	544
52 In the cross of Christ I glory	70	336	104	416	195	157		409	134	183
52 Watchman tell us of the night		440		358	149	109				
54 O Christ our hope, our heart's desire							146	144		
54 Disposer supreme							506	178	654	788
54 O Holy Spirit Lord of grace							231	453		
54 O what their joy		589	337		424	310	281	465	349	
54A Bethlehem, of noblest cities		48					76	40		
54 O Love how deep, how broad		344	88		518*	150	187	459	63	62
54 Christ is made		348	367	298	433	263	620	170	237	7*
54 All glory, laud and honour	39	62	108	424	187		598	622	120	84
54 Jerusalem the golden		597	347	303	428	309	278	412	352	652
54 Come ye faithful		94	132	448	205	186	133	131	140	
54 The day of Resurrection		96	141	437	208		132	137	141	208
54 Christian dost thou see them		556		238	360	364	91	72	484	
55 Now that the daylight		159	268			‡	1	254		
54 On Jordan's bank		10	36			115	50	9	73	
55 As with gladness		52	82	397	174	119	79	39	95	132
55 Come ye thankful people	233	137	407	522	525	461	482	289	645	962
55 Abide with me	217	467	272	289	64	209	27	363	622	948
55 Our God our help	223	289	320	28	111	1	165	450	52	878
55 O come all ye faithful	81	12	45	386	170	132	59	28	85	118
55 O come, O come, Immanuel	78	2	34	354	147	110	49	8	72	257
55 Holy Holy Holy	1	266	165	26	11	251	160	162	223	36
55 Lead kindly light		430		272	331	215	298	425	509	612
55 Hark the herald	83	27	60	388	163	120	60	24	84	117
55 Forty days and forty nights		55				148	92	73		165
55 O sacred head	105	75	116	418	194	170	111	102	127	202
56 Within the churchyard							575‡			
56 There is a green hill		65	114	414	202	171	214	106	136	180
56 Once in royal David's city		236			462		432	605	89	859
56 All things bright		311		34	456	478	442	587	684	851
56 For all the saints	144	126	174	536	425	306	527	641	363	832
56 For the beauty of the earth	54	296	561	35	2	66	171	309	37	35
56 The church's one foundation	236	396	369	297	434	260	255	489	254	701
57 See the conqueror mounts		103					148	145		
57 O thou not made with hands		(491)					259	464	550	707

	B	H	L	M	P	Pm	A	E	C	M
57 At even when the sun was set		168		501	55	55	20	266	632	689
57 Breathe on me Breath of God	317	375	488	133	235	233	236	76*	216	300
57 Our blest Redeemer		368					230	157	209	283
57 Just as I am	187	409	296	119	272	319	3	316	385	353
57 At the name of Jesus	363	356	179	76	143	197	225	368	167	249
57 Now thank we all our God	234	276	533	49	9	29	379	533	42	10
57 If thou but suffer God	(203)	211*	453	210	344	83			389	(504)
57 Praise to the Lord, the Almighty	10	(279)	543	55	1	15	382	536	45	64
57 Ein feste burg	37	551	229	20	91	363	183	362	485	494
59 The King of love	215	345	456	67	106	79	197	490	61	76
59 Bright the vision that delighted							161	372	16	(25)
59 Alleluia, sing to Jesus			158				399	301		
59 O worship the Lord in the beauty						31	77	42	275	9
59 The day thou gavest		179	274	500	59	48	33	277	626	667
59 REGENT SQUARE	87	28	50	66	168	263	279	431	18	12
59 IRBY		236			462		432	605	89	859
59 ST ALBINUS		88					140	134	147	216
59 LANCASHIRE	237	553	495	342	208	192				245
59 PRAISE MY SOUL		282	549	18	31	16	365	470	18	12
59 Onward Christian Soldiers	393	557	509	305	350	382	629	643	527	822
59 Fight the good fight	394	560	461	240	359	367	304	389	512	490
61 Guide me	202	205*	343	271	339	93	296	397	500	615
61 HYFRYDOL	11	479	315	132	123	13	260	301	179	380
61 LLANGLOFFAN			430	260	511	436		207	398	330
61 ABERYSTWYTH	20	440	91	125	216	211		87	473	726
61 EBENEZER	340	519	233	242	361	441		108	442	616
61 JOANNA (ST. DENIO)	32	301	526	27	85	7	372	407	28	34
61 GWALCHMAI		95				65	367	424	426	23
61 LLANFAIR	115	104	128	443	4	19	147	143	20	205
61 RHOSYMEDRE		504	94			169		303		
62 BRYN CALFARIA	121		156	364	90	291		319		324
63 AMAZING GRACE	165		448	92	275					
68 Ah, holy Jesus		71	123	412	191	163		70	775	177
68 The duteous day		181	276			53	34	278	629	
68 Rejoice, O Lord		520				430	582	475	571	882
68 All my hope		183*				339	3*	73*	417	70
68 City of God		386			436	261	258	375	253	703
68 I look to thee in every need				219	114	92		406		
68 My faith looks up	382	449	479	143	378	348		439	479	238
68 Jesu thou joy of loving hearts	72	485	356	329	215	290	387		291	109
68 Immortal love	329	360		157	229	230	208	408	186	102
68 Dear Lord and Father	270	435	506	235	416	341	184	383	408	669

119

	B	H	L	M	P	Pm	A	E	C	M
68 O brother man		493		199	474	410			541	901
71 O Lord and Master		501				224		456	186	103
73 Eternal Ruler		200*	373			275	20*	384	554	892
73 It came upon the midnight	86		54	390	160	129	66	26	88	130
73 O little town	85		41	381	171	134	65	15	718	125
73 The day thou gavest		179	274	500	59	48	33	277	626	667
73 Jesu good above all other		322					45*	598	464	
74 Hail thee festival day (tune)		86	142				110*	624		
74 God be with you (tune)		490		540	78	61		524	678	914
74 For all the saints	144	126	174	536	425	306	527	641	363	832
74 Come down O love divine		376	508	466		239	235	152	204	273
74 Immortal love	329	360		157	229	230	208	408	186	201
74 Once to every man and nation	385	519		242	361	441		563		898
74 City of God		386			436	261	258	375	253	703
74 O little town	85		41	381	171	134	65	15	718	125
74 Dear Lord and Father	270	435	506	235	416	341	184	383	408	669
74 Judge eternal		518	418	546	517	435		423	572	883
74 O God of earth and altar		521	428	484	511	436		562	578	
75 Praise to the Lord	10	(279)	543	55	1	15	382	536	45	64
75 Let all the world		290		10	22		375	427	3	5
75 King of glory							367	424	426	23
75 Teach me, my God and King						401	337	485	433	597
75 Come, my Way, my Truth		196*	513							12*
75 Will thou forgive that sin		123*						515		
75 In this world							Songs of Praise 348			
75 My soul there is a country							286	82*	356	466
75 Most glorious Lord of life							283	602		
75 My song is love unknown	486	217*	94			169	102	27*	128	144
75 Abide with me	217	467	272	289	64	209	27	363	622	948
75 Lead kindly light		430		272	331	215	298	425	509	612
75 Praise to the Holiest		343					185	471	71	74
76 Give me, O Christ									532	
76 Almighty Father who for us									564	
76 Christ is the world's true light		258			492	198	13*	101*	171	9*
Not for prayer							68*			
76 Kings Weston	363	356	179	76	143	197		368		
76 LOVE UNKNOWN		217*					102	27*	128	144
76 ABBOTS LEIGH		208*	405*		384*		257	48*	243	42*
85 They'll know we are Christians		35*			619*					
88 LASST UNS ERFIEVEN	9	599	143	19	34	12	199*	519	31	4
88 CHRISTE SANCTORUM		157	169	504	43	41	10	165	588	8*
88 O what their joy		589	337		424	310	281	465	349	

	B	H	L	M	P	Pm	A	E	C	M
88 O come all ye faithful	81	12	45	386	170	132	59	28	85	118
89 There's a wideness	171	304	290	69	110	101	364	499	369	318
89 My God, how wonderful thou art		284	524				169	441	24	73
89 O come and mourn		74			192	164	113	111	135	187
89 Hark, hark, my soul		472			426		354	399		651
89 Faith of our fathers	143	393	500	151	348	365				402
90 Tantum ergo		199					383	326		63
90 O salutaris		209					394	330		
90 Reap me the earth		Cantate Domino				871	Praise the Lord: 62			

DATE DUE

HIGHSMITH 45-220